TO KILL
THE KING

POST-TRADITIONAL
GOVERNANCE AND BUREAUCRACY

DAVID JOHN FARMER

M.E.Sharpe
Armonk, New York
London, England

Library of Congress Cataloging-in-Publication Data

Farmer, David John, 1935–
    To kill the king : post-traditional governance and bureaucracy / by David
John Farmer.
        p. cm.
Includes bibliographical references and index.
ISBN 0-7656-1480-4 (cloth: alk. paper) — ISBN 0-7656-1481-2 (pbk.: alk. paper)
    1. Public administration. 2. Corporate governance. 3. Bureaucracy. I. Title.

JF1351.F373 2005
351'.01—dc22
                                                                              2004017168

Printed in the United States of America

The paper used in this publication meets the minimum requirements of
American National Standard for Information Sciences
Permanence of Paper for Printed Library Materials,
ANSI Z 39.48-1984.

                                    ∞

BM (c)   10   9   8   7   6   5   4   3   2   1
BM (p)   10   9   8   7   6   5   4   3   2   1

To David and Tyler,

the next generation

Imagination is not a gift usually associated
with bureaucracies.

—*9/11 National Commission*

Contents

Preface

Imagine inaugurating for the rule of imagination in governance. Let's create a post-traditional consciousness that can revitalize governance and bureaucracy. Let's explore constitutive features of this fresh consciousness that privileges the imagination.

Post-traditional consciousness of public and private governance is not the bastard son of traditional consciousness. Nor is it a daughter who grew up to do better than her mother. The substantive relationship of post-traditional consciousness to the traditional has been marginal. Post-traditional attitudes preceded the traditional, parallel to the sense where Jean-Francois Lyotard speaks of the postmodern as preceding the modern. They are also concurrent with, and subsequent to, the traditional. Post-traditional thinking about governance and bureaucracy should not be described in terms of (in opposition to, as a supplement to) traditional thinking. It stands by itself. It should be described in its own terms. To make an analogy: when exploring physics, it is neither necessary nor desirable to start with alchemy.

These essays on post-traditional consciousness of governance and bureaucracy must speak to the reader in an open voice that is outside traditional parameters. The writing voice is intended to invite open engagement from the reader, all in the interest of achieving post-traditional consciousness. The voice emphasizes the larger picture, some extradisciplinary metaphors, and some foreign ideas. The voice's character is expected to shift for the reader as she continues reading the essays; and the meaning of earlier essays is anticipated to alter as others are read. Adapting a 1992 American election slogan, I have to remind myself; it's the consciousness, stupid.

These essays have relevance for disciplines like political science and economics and for action fields like public administration and business administration. More precisely, they are relevant to those significant parts that bear on governance. They have special interest for reformers who work within the more important of these disciplines and fields. Two changes are among those suggested for these subjects. The first is the new consciousness. The second is that the subjects transcend, in the way that will be explained, current disciplinary constraints.

I expect the essays to be of special interest in public administration and related thinking. I have long hoped to contribute toward the creation of a fresh, not merely a reformulated, field of public administration. But the post-traditional ideas in these essays are intended no less for the other governance disciplines and fields.

Post-traditional thinking has been nourished in my case by discussions among scholars who constitute the Public Administration Theory Network (PAT-Net), an American-based association with a membership that extends to countries on other continents. The network was created in 1978 as a result of dissatisfaction with the platitudes and inertia of traditional public administration thinking and practice. It flourishes today. Within the theory network there are many divergent views. PAT-Net has been very generous in supporting and encouraging me to play with ideas. Members have talked to me, listened to me, and given me intellectual and emotional support. For example, I write a column called CommonSense@Admin for the association's journal, *Administrative Theory & Praxis*. Many of the ideas in these essays were born in that column and in other articles. I have repeated and developed some of my ideas and materials. The account of post-traditional thinking, justice, and practice in this collection of essays is my own. But it owes its life to the support, inspiration, and brilliance of members of that association.

Thanks for comments on drafts of this book from O.C. McSwite (nom de plume of Orion F. White and Cynthia J. McSwain), Rosemary L. Farmer, and Patricia M. Patterson. Thanks also to editor Harry Briggs.

Introduction

Imagine that the 9/11 National Commission on Terrorist Attacks upon the United States is right in highlighting the importance of imagination. It speaks about institutionalizing imagination. "It is therefore crucial to find a way of routinizing, even bureaucratizing, the exercise of imagination" (9/11 Commission, 344). Imagine imagination pervading all of governance for all major aims, as much as for government outwitting terrorism. Imagine that an adequate sense of imagination is more than merely connecting dots. What would be required for such a reign of imagination? I suggest that this rule of imagination requires post-traditional governance and bureaucracy.

These essays suggest constitutive features of post-traditional governance and bureaucracy. They reflect on a fresh consciousness that can help us live together better. They seek to answer three general questions. First, what is post-traditional thinking? Second, what is post-traditional justice? Third, what is post-traditional practice? The essays discuss thinking as playing, justice as seeking, and practice as art. They culminate in a recommendation to kill the king.

Three Questions

I describe each of the three questions in preliminary terms, sketch an intellectual context, and indicate the contents of the essays.

Thinking as Play: What Is Post-Traditional Thinking?

Post-traditional thinking as playing is fresh awareness of what is critical. It gains its creative energy, its scholarly dynamism, from much that traditional governance thinking represses and, misguidedly, considers unimportant.

Post-traditional thinking as playing seeks to emphasize, for example, radically imaginative thinking throughout governance. The 9/11 Commission report (2004, 339), just mentioned, spoke of four kinds of failures in government: "in imagination, policy, capabilities, and management." Featured first was lack of imagination. It is agreed that the 9/11 Commission has a narrow view of imagination and of the break with tradition that the radically imaginative presents. Imagination at its fullest is not about mere technical capabilities. It is about developing a post-traditional consciousness throughout governance, public and private. Radical imagination has a negligible chance of flourishing in a seedbed of traditional thinking. It requires thinking that is independent of the traditional.

Post-traditional thinking/feeling, above all, is reflection and dialogue that is radically open. It is always open, always searching. The meaning of radical openness is suggested in the features described in the first part of the book, the first six essays. Yet the openness goes further, and its description continues throughout the other two parts. Post-traditional thinking, for example, is permeated by the justice as seeking that is described in the second part. It is also infused by the practice as art discussed in the third part. It is open in method; for example, it accepts that the barriers between the aesthetic, the scientific, and the normative crumble (see Habermas, 1983, 9). It is open in aim: for instance, the fresh consciousness sought is not a unified or single vision.

Justice as Seeking: What Is Post-Traditional Justice?

Post-traditional thinking is moral reflection. Yet there is a difference. "Moral" in this case doesn't include justice thinking as it is traditionally understood in governance and bureaucratic contexts. Post-traditional justice involves a consciousness generated by a shift in citizen-citizen relations from the hierarchical (the closed, the semiclosed) to the truly horizontal (the truly open). There is a shift from an authoritarian toward a lateral basis for justice determinations. In government, a parallel shift would be one away from primary reliance on a top-down relationship from political leaders to citizens. The movement in justice as seeking is toward primary reliance on the self in lateral relations with other selves.

This openness in justice as seeking is consistent with a sense that there is something wrong, in the governance and bureaucratic contexts at least, with justice thinking as we have inherited it. Justice as seeking stands against justice thinking that is too constrained in its self-consciousness. It resists thinking that is too limited in considering philosophical style and lived experiences. Contemporary professional moral philosophizing, much as I may love it, is too confined within a single disciplinary tradition. Traditional justice thinking stops short in its recognition of the complexities of concrete historical and cultural situations. It proceeds as if the universe of moral practice could be completely captured by the rational, the known, and the ahistorical—by the cognitive, the neat, and the abstract. It is as if the stochastic pressures of pain, power, and finitude—as if the world's random constrictions, oppressions, paradoxes, contradictions, and surely absurdities—could be discounted.

Justice invites radical openness in seeking. Consider the openness of the formal meaning of justice, for example. "Justice" as a concept can be understood—initially at least—to refer to that part of ethics that concerns the minimum that each person should consider that she owes to other persons, not as a matter of law, love, politeness, or prudence but of what morally ought to be the case. Ethical judgments not dealing with relationships with others are outside the scope of justice. On the one hand, it seems clear that justice, as a matter of minimum ethical or moral obligation, is concerned with what person X should consider that she owes to person Y. It is concerned with what, morally, person Y should expect from person X. On the other hand, even this traditional view— that justice is the minimum that each person should consider that she owes to other people, as a matter of what morally ought to be the case—is open to question. One distinguished moral philosopher, Elizabeth Anscombe, confidently asserts "'Justice' I have no idea how to define, except that its sphere is that of actions which relate to someone else" (1958). She describes justice solely by specifying its sphere, that is, actions relating to other people.

Yet another philosopher can show that even this limited island of apparent closure is really open. Cupit (1966) denies Anscombe's claim that treatment of one person by another is an essential factor, and he points to the claim that animals and trees can be considered to be owed certain justice obligations.

Practice as Art: What Is Post-Traditional Practice?

Post-traditional governance practice should be an art, where the artistry turns toward the truly human. By truly human, I mean where each and every individual is treated in her fullest human dimensions (psycho, socio, bio, spiritual, and other dimensions)—treated as if each person were an artist in the conduct of her own life. Post-traditional practice should be more like an art with this human aim, where practitioners carry out their activities as if they were each creating a work of art. Recall that, when speaking about ancient Greek ethics, Michel Foucault speaks of a person leading (and justifying) an "ethical" life as if she were a work of art. I am thinking in a parallel way for post-traditional governance practice as art, which includes post-traditional thinking as playing and justice as seeking. A function of post-traditional thinking and ethics is to provide the space for such practitioner artistry.

None of this means that governance will have no muscle, no barbed wire. I imagine that neither a mass murderer nor a white-collar criminal, for example, should be merely coddled, read poetry, and shown paintings. Post-traditional thinking as playing and justice as seeking will suggest how practice as art, in different contexts, can best aim toward treating all humans more like humans —and for humans to be more human.

Intellectual Context

Governance and its bureaucracy cannot be discussed adequately without the thinker going outside her discipline(s) or field(s), without adventuring in the turfs of a range of foreign specialties. Governance is understood widely, for example, to include ways in which political, economic, and administrative power and authority should be experienced. The scope required is larger than is available in a truncated field like political science, economics, or the administrative specializations—public administration, business administration, hotel administration, sports administration, travel administration, and so on. For example, I think that it is impossible to reflect adequately on politics or bureaucracy without thinking about economics; it is not possible to reflect adequately on economics without thinking about politics and bureaucracy. In essay #2, I describe the ideal scope as including not only these specializations but also subjects like philosophy, sociology, social work, literature, arts, and other turfs related to the biological, psychological, the social, and the spiritual. Looking out from within a narrow specialization distorts what is seen and makes it virtually impossible to present the larger picture that is needed. The situation is more complicated yet. The thinker has to understand deviant traditions within each discipline or field, and it helps to have experienced the gut feelings of being in the practice trenches. The governance thinker, and reader, should venture beyond narrow specialist confines. I have a suggestion in essay #2 about how this should be done.

Political economy in the days of Adam Smith was a moral science, and it was Smith's plan to write a trilogy that encompasses not only his *Wealth of Nations* and *Theory of Moral Sentiments* but also his work on government. Unlike in Smith's day, regrettably now the social science disciplines are hyperconstricted. In the spirit of Adam Smith, this book steps outside the prison of a single contemporary discipline.

Contents

It is suggested that the reader read the essays in whichever order she pleases. There is a story that emanates from the order presented, and I would read it that way. But it is not necessary. Another alternative is to go through the three sections in turn, but reading the essays in reverse order. That is, the reader could start with Essay 6 and then read the essays in reverse order to 1. Then she could restart at Essay 12 and read the essays in reverse order to 7, and restart again at 18 and go back essay-by-essay to 13.

Part I: Thinking as Play

Essays 1 through 6 speak to constitutive features of a radically open and fresh consciousness that is post-traditional thinking as playing. This consciousness privileges the human and is sensitive to context. In explaining, I try to practice what is preached.

Essay 1 explains that the best escape route out of the traditional bureaucratic doldrums is thinking as playing. Forget the misleading dream of a science of governance; forget the nightmare of tinkering. Play at its highest level is poetic contemplation that begins in imagination and focuses on constitutive patterns of imaginative possibilities. Start with Plato.

Essay 2 explains that thinkers as players-with-a-purpose should be gadflies, as long as that includes the spirit of disinterested and poetic contemplation. A first ideal in a gadfly mission should be privileging broad-brush governance concerns, with a consequent need to match topics with new turf. A second ideal in a gadfly mission is the inclusion of voices that are excluded from or pushed to the margins in traditional discussions about governance.

Essay 3 explains that thinking as playing should aim to clear space for each individual self to achieve her fullest potential. Attention is invited to the whole person-in-herself in-her-difference. It is also directed to the contested character of the self, pointing to the self as detritus of relevant language.

Essay 4 explains that all thinkers are institutionalized; the question is what to do about it. I recommend that post-traditional thinkers should be conscious about both individual and group signatures. I favor recognizing links between what is written and the life of the thinker. I suggest starting from the edge of the group's paradigm or from the in-between space between paradigms.

Essay 5 explains that thinking as playing should be sensitive to symbols and symbolic systems.

Essay 6 explains that skepticism is coherent, as in the form exhibited by the life of Sextus Empiricus. While not committed to skepticism, thinking as playing should be sensitive to limits in knowing. It can distinguish between Big T Truths and what-counts-as-true. What-counts-as-true is limited by language and coshaped by unthoughts. Thinking as playing should anticipate aporia.

Part II: Justice as Seeking

Essays 7 through 12 suggest constitutive features of post-traditional justice as seeking wisdom. They describe the seeking as ongoing and as extending beyond established parameters.

Essay 7 suggests that we should acknowledge our legacy for justice-seeking. There is aporia. There is a will-to-simplicity. Also part of our legacy is the centrality in much public ethics of capitalism.

Essay 8 suggests that justice-seeking should avoid canned solutions. Justice systems are indecisive, for example, if one seeks conclusive, rational evidence that any one system is *the* right system. Indecisiveness is also reflected in meta-ethics and in the so-called hermeneutic turn. This is also our legacy.

Essay 9 suggests that searching within my self is a critical part of justice thinking, both for humans and for human organizations. Yet it is difficult partly because what is within is socially constructed. Create my own style, which Nietzsche describes as shaping values. Recognize that this is a reciprocal movement between the self and the other.

Essay 10 suggests that empathy for the other should include authentic hesitation in justice-claiming. This is suggested both for individuals and for organizations. Such hesitation can take such forms as empathy of silence or empathy of listening. Authentic hesitation is in a long tradition of neighboring ideas in political philosophy.

Essay 11 suggests that traditional insights, when open-ended, facilitate justice as seeking wisdom. The Golden Rule is discussed as an example. It is popular, but ignored by most modern philosophers. It emphasizes the "I" in determining the relationship of governance to the other and to the expanding sphere of altruism.

Essay 12 suggests that seeking justice wisdom from literatures in other cultural traditions should be the rule rather than the exception. As an example, contrast Confucianism and Christianity in their attitudes toward hesitancy and assertiveness.

Part III: Practice as Art

Essays 13 through 18 indicate constitutive features of post-traditional practice as art. They describe the post-traditional practitioner as an artist. They explain what is meant by, symbolically, killing the king. Several themes recur, like power-over, human individuals, machine systems, and the invisible hand. Above all, there is the theme of resymbolization.

Essay 13 indicates that practitioners should be artists. Practice as art should include thinking as playing and justice as seeking. Beyond this, practice as art should engage the day-to-day with concern about the relationship between the totality of political, economic, and administrative systems and the individual human. The art of governance should seek to kill the king. One face of the king is the view of governance as a matter of machine systems and technicism.

Essay 14 indicates that practice as art should seek the longer-run termination of the cult of the leader. As long as it values leadership, governance should embrace the art of just, rather than heroic, leadership. The cult of the leader is systemic. It is a systemic feature of the symbolic repertoire of what counts as the civilizing process in society. The examples focus mainly on the visible hand of leadership in traditional government, especially in public bureaucracy; but the conclusions apply throughout governance.

Essay 15 indicates that practice as art should engage the rhetoric of economics. Attention is drawn to the symbolic functioning of the invisible hand and of economic theory as a whole. It is also directed to economic corporations. This essay focuses on non-traditional government.

Essay 16 indicates that the art of governance should recognize the barbs in systems and the pivotal role of society in creating the barbed wire. Barbed wire, symbolizing the combination of beneficial and hurtful effect, is discussed in terms of prevalence, types, and unraveling. Immigration and corrections are examples.

Essay 17 indicates that the post-traditional practitioner should be motivated as a regulative ideal by love rather than by mere efficiency. It should embrace unengineering as a symbol.

Essay 18 indicates of faith in the ideal (or ideology) of a citizen turn. This is illustrated in terms of political hierarchy, noting that both hierarchical democracy and open democracy present aporia. Re-symbolization is suggested to nourish the impulse that the existence of hierarchy is not the norm that needs no evidence, but a deviation that requires justification. Executing the king requires changing symbolic systems in citizens' heads.

I

Thinking as Play

The play's the thing,
Wherein I'll catch the conscience of the king.

—*Shakespeare, Hamlet*

What Is Post-Traditional Thinking?

Post-traditional thinking/feeling aims for an open and fresh consciousness. This consciousness is constituted by play that privileges the human and that is sensitive to context. Thinking as playing is described as *the* escape route from the intellectual and performance doldrums of traditional governance.

The first two essays focus on the nature of thinking as playing. The next two concentrate on play privileging the human. The last two essays concern thinking as playing being sensitive to a context that includes symbolism and aporia. Aporia is "being at a loss, puzzled, stumped, stymied."

1 • Start with Plato: Playing

The best escape route out of the traditional bureaucratic doldrums is thinking as playing. Forget the misleading dream of a science of governance; forget the nightmare of tinkering. Play at its highest level is poetic contemplation that begins in imagination and that focuses on constitutive patterns of imaginative possibilities. Start with Plato.

> . . . all philosophy has its origins in wonder.
>
> —*Plato*

Imagine that administration is not like a machine. The idea of the *machinery of government* is so culturally ingrained that it's hard to imagine this. It's been a given throughout much of the past four or five hundred years. Isaac Newton and other scientific thinkers were able to work their marvels partly because they conceptualized the universe as mechanical. By viewing the universe as a mere machine operating without theological intervention, those thinkers could develop important life-changing explanations. This view of the universe as mechanical reached a zenith in the eighteenth-century Enlightenment, and it was reflected in politics and in other aspects of life. The American Founding Fathers saw government in large part as mechanical, for example, and they developed a machinery of government that boasted features similar to a well-running, now-old-fashioned watch—like a Constitution replete with checks and balances. Since the Einsteinian and other revolutions of twentieth-century science, today the idea of the universe as a mere machine has less of a grip. Yet we still see much evidence of the machine view, as when many physicians treat us as if our bodies were mere machines. When American public administration was created in the latter part of the nineteenth century, it's no surprise that the machine model was the way that governmental administration was conceptualized. Don't misunderstand: I'm not saying that the machine has been the only model. I am suggesting that, even when another metaphor like a living plant is used, it is difficult to imagine that administration doesn't operate basically like a machine or a quasi-machine. Imagine that administration is like something else, like a set of colors or a pattern of libidinal pulses, or none of these. Imagine that it is like a combination, part like this and part like that. Imagine that it is like this one day and like that the other. Imagine that it is like nothing else. Although it's hard to go against the grain, imagine that bureaucracy is not machinery.

This is a first of some ten examples I give of *constitutive patterns of imaginative possibilities* that are clearly within the traditional turf of public administration. These constitutive patterns are designs or paradigms or metaphors or models that constitute actual or possible states of affairs, as I will explain later. The patterns are part of the most important kind of *thinking as playing*.

In this essay, I describe this one kind of play, and I suggest that the best escape route out of traditional bureaucratic and governance doldrums is thinking that includes this kind of playing. The kind is where the benefit is indirect; it is play with no immediate purpose. In two sentences, this kind of play is poetic contemplation that, like all play, begins in imagination. What should be contemplated are these constitutive patterns of imaginative possibilities. Essay 2 speaks of another kind, play with a direct purpose—and it gives examples outside the traditional boundary lines of public administration. Paradoxically, it's only through *inclusion* of contemplation not committed to producing practical results—through play with no immediate purpose—that we can enjoy the quantum leap in practical insights that we should have.

For example number two of a constitutive pattern: *imagine that administration is not top-down or hierarchical, relying on direction, coordination, and control from above.* Let's call what is imagined *open administration*. This imagining is complicated in at least two ways. First, imaginations will differ on what this open administration looks like, although the general direction seems clear enough. There is a range of openness that extends from just short of a hierarchical extreme, where arrangements and individuals are maximally directed, coordinated, and controlled. It extends through intermediate positions of openness to the other extreme, where arrangements are maximally open. This range could be similar to a market structure where a spectrum of options would run from the maximally monopolistic through degrees of oligopoly to perfect competition. But it's not as simple as it sounds. Recall the position held by many anarchists, for example, favoring a society without a government but with rules. As another example, it's not a huge stretch to imagine intermediate forms, like networks of transient hierarchies, functioning in a way analogous to rules in the anarchist case. Imagine a transient hierarchy in terms of Pete and Pat trapped in a cave and wanting to escape. If Pat gives instructions simply because both believe that in this particular circumstance she knows best how to get out, that relationship can be described as a transient hierarchy. It's a different matter if Pat takes charge because there is an explicit or implicit rule that makes "Pat is boss" habitual in Pete-Pat transactions or because it is her right. Second among the difficulties is that it is hard to buck the everyday evidence of the existence of massive vertical structures. Our inherited habits of mind tend to confuse what is socially constructed with what is natural. Although it's hard to go against this grain, imagine administration that is not top-down.

Examples 3–7: Imagine that administration is not dominated so thoroughly by the symbolic system of the economy. Imagine that administration harbors no ethic of mere efficiency. Or imagine the opposite; imagine that administration embraces instrumental rationality even more fully. Imagine that administration is not infused by the professional model. Imagine (again) that administration is not typically reified, treated as if it were a natural kind. Imagine that administration is not group administration.

Examples 8–10: Imagine all of these changes together, and more. Imagine that in this way we can transform the status quo; imagine that we can kill the king! Then, imagine—play with ideas about—what possible worlds this imagining opens.

Governance is worth contemplating, playfully.

> Lifetime is a child playing draughts;
> the kingship belongs to the child.
>
> —*Heraclitus*

This theory of thinking as play relies on interpretations of play that have fascinated an important stream of thinkers since Heraclitus at the dawn of Western philosophy. Also, it continues my own writing such as *Public Administration Discourse as Play with a Purpose* (1998, 37–56) that sketched modern and postmodern views of administrative play. It's not about play in the sense of the business of organized games in Little League baseball, or even in the subjective terms of Immanuel Kant. Rather, it's about play as a mode of being. As I explained, the features that Hans Gadamer identifies in an ontology of play include a naturalness: a to-and-fro movement (e.g., as in the play of forces, the play of fountains); a movement that's unconnected with a goal and that renews itself in repetition; a relation with an other, human or nonhuman; losing its purpose unless the player loses herself in her play; a risky activity (the player can be trapped by the fascination of the play!); an activity that has a closed character (the more it's done for an audience, the less it's play—whether in sporting or religious play!); and a "lack of consciousness in the playing consciousness, which makes it absolutely impossible to decide between belief and nonbelief" (Gadamer, 1975, 96). It's about an understanding of play that rises to John Huizinga's view of the human as a "playing animal" and to Schiller's scintillating claim that "man is only truly himself when he is at play."

The point of this play is a fresh consciousness, replacing traditional, bankrupting attitudes in bureaucratic thinking. The fresh consciousness, for one thing, stands against a traditional bureaucratic attitude of anti-intellectualism. Take public administration, for example. *I know* is how O.C. McSwite (1997, 174) characterizes a traditional attitude "produced by the anti-intellectualism of certainty." It's a whistling-in-the-dark attitude that defends current malpractice.

> The heaviest element yet known to science was recently discovered by investigators at a major U.S. research university. The new element, tentatively named administratium, . . . is inert. However, it . . . impedes every reaction it comes into contact with . . . (A)dministratium . . . (concentrates) at certain points such as government agencies, large corporations and universities. . . .
>
> —*DeBuwitz*

This fresh consciousness stands against a narrow conception of the function of bureaucratic studies as limited essentially to upgrading the machinery, for example, as in machinery of government. Instead, the fresh consciousness wants to face a central problem of governance in our emergent society. The problem is the dead hand of bureaucracy that contaminates and soils—or, in DeBuwitz's story above, the prevalence of administratium. (DeBuwitz, 1989, characterizes administratium as a chemical element consisting of one neutron, 125 assistant neutrons, 75 vice neutrons, and 111 assistant vice neutrons—312 particles that change places and are held together by a force called morons.) By dead hand of bureaucracy or administratium, I mean that complex of constitutive features that frustrates the best of societal intentions. For liberals, it's the dead hand that makes it difficult to implement grand schemes of social justice without incorporating bureaucratic features that corrupt and spoil. For neoconservatives, it's the dead hand that persuades that the only sensible response is to starve the beast. It's a dead hand that, encountering the mole of human aspiration, can contribute materially to bringing down great empires as different as the Roman and the Soviet. It's a dead hand that could yet frustrate the hopes of those who want the United States or the European Union to succeed—and more. It's the dead hand that perversely can prompt the traditional thinker to list the many benefits, the real benefits, of bureaucracy. The fresh consciousness, instead, embraces the dead hand within bureaucracy as a prime philosophical and policy problem of our emerging times.

Claim #1

> Poetry is a sort of truancy, a dream within the dream of life, a wild flower planted among our wheat.
>
> —*Oakeshott*

Claim #1, then, is that the most important kind of play is poetic contemplation that begins in imagination, and such play should be at the center of post-traditional thinking. For geeks and lovers of wisdom, this will evoke Plato's (and, after him, Aristotle's) famous and beautiful claim that the love of wisdom—philosophy—has its origins in wonder. By *begins,* I mean what primarily energizes, drives, inspires. By *begins in imagination,* I mean what is needed for such thinking to flourish. Playful thinking may be prompted by a variety of desires, for example, for more service, for more justice, for more quality of life. The thinking may engage the imagination, or not. Absent imagination or poetry, thinking is not play.

By *contemplation,* I mean the usual sense of meditating or musing about something deeply, focusing on being open to yet-unrecognized possibilities and to yet-hidden nuances of meanings. This meditating or musing can be done individually or in dialogue with others. But there are degrees of better and worse contemplation. I mean contemplation that is exemplary when it is imaginative or poetic, attending poetically to meanings below the surface.

By *imaginative* or *poetic,* I mean more than thinking outside of the box—trite, hackneyed phrase. I do mean to include thought experiments, including those conducted deep in the plushest of armchairs. Economic theorists, theoretical physicists, philosophers, and others attempt them, almost routinely. Isaac Newton's famous thought experiments about absolute space and absolute motion included his actually hanging up water buckets on ropes—as well as a thought experiment where "two globes . . . (are) tied together with a cord and then twirled about their center of gravity" (Sorensen, 1992,

146). Yet, I mean to emphasize thought experiments that are more than merely a matter of being imaginative in rationalizing. I mean to include not only a more vigorous but also a more independent role for the play of the imagination. Notice below Andre Breton's description in his First Surrealist Manifesto of the role of imagination. Notice Carl Jung's understanding of the play of the imagination as independent—as independent as is reflected in Taoist and other systems of meditation. Recall the poets of the imagination, like John Keats. "Beauty is truth, truth beauty—that is all / Ye know on earth, and all ye need to know." I mean to include in poetic contemplation what Michael Oakeshott describes (1991, 451) writing of poetic contemplation as a sort of truancy, a dream within the dream of life, a wildflower planted among our wheat.

Claim #2

Claim #2 is that the most important kind of play should contemplate constitutive patterns of imaginative possibilities. By *constitutive patterns,* I have said that I include designs or paradigms or models or metaphors or stories that constitute parts of what is or what might be. I also mean incomplete and vague understandings of such designs. Begin by thinking of a constitutive pattern as being similar to a chemical formula that constitutes an explosion (e.g., $e = mc^2$) or the design that shapes a remodeling of a house. I do not think of patterns as grounding what is above, but I do imagine them as being underneath the surface of what is or what might be.

By such patterns of *imaginative possibilities,* I mean constitutive features that make, create, sustain, or account for a possible state of affairs. Constitutive patterns of imaginative possibilities are at least figments of contemplation and at best figments of poetic contemplation. They imagine possibilities beyond traditional understandings of the present, the past, and the future.

Play and Prescription

The best escape route out of the traditional bureaucratic and governance doldrums is thinking as playing. Forget the misleading dream of a science of governance topics; it is a false prescription. Escape the nightmare of mere tinkering, mere pragmatic prescriptivism!

Prescribing Play

Otto Neurath is wrong, and right, in his striking metaphor of the ship. He is wrong to the extent that he assumes that knowledge that improves society is nothing like play. He is wrong to the extent that he assumes that such knowledge must be, say, science that is prescriptive. Neurath likens creating relevant knowledge to rebuilding a ship in the open sea. As he writes, "We are like sailors who have to rebuild their ship in the open sea, without ever being able to dismantle it in dry dock and reconstruct it from the best components" (Nemeth & Stadler, 2002). He was a political scientist, a sociologist, an antiphilosopher, a logical positivist, and a believer in the unity of science; his metaphor speaks to all governance fields. The ship metaphor is right about some things, for example, he would say right about inheriting a world-as-it-is in motion and about the antifoundational nature of knowing. Yet, that society (or governance) resembles a ship does not entail that all thinkers have to think as if they were sailors currently at sea. Not all people working for a ship need be on board, for example, ocean liner companies employ many landlubbers. Even onboard sailors can contemplate relevant issues broader than the ship they are sailing on, for example, about oceanography, meteorology, and even ship design. When substituting steel for wood and diesel for sail, the designers of steel and diesel ships need not serve on wooden sailing ships in motion. Neurath's ship is a nice metaphor, but it is linear rhetoric.

We remain in the grip of linear rhetoric, and play wants to escape this. Plato invites us in his *Republic* (509d) to imagine a line that divides knowledge and opinion, distinguishing what is really real from what is not. What rhetoric! He wants his reader to know that the top type of thinking is always better. That is, he wants us to assume that his line is the right way up. He asks us to ascend the line. Play beckons the reader toward nonlinear contexts that, under specified conditions, can treat even the expression of opinion as more fruitful than the assertion of knowledge. These conditions may be where opinion is understood to be mere opinion, and (see Essay 6) where the limits of knowing are recognized. This can be illustrated in terms of economic theory. Typically, mainstream economics does not recognize theorizing as the playing it could become. Many theorists think as if they were dealing with (see Essay 6) the truth, the whole truth, and nothing but the truth—and, oddly, some become cynical.

In the same rhetorical spirit and for definitional purposes, imagine a line divided into two parts and showing two levels of thinking. In the top half is thinking constituted by varieties of play, and in the bottom half is thinking that is not playful. In the top half would be much hermeneutics, some positivism and little tinkering. Hermeneutics (interpretation) refers to understandings, and positivism refers to explanations. Both understandings and explanations are used in the same senses as in philosophy of science; the former includes meanings and normative judgments, for instance, and the latter does not. Play is as described in Essays 1 through 6. At its highest level, it is for its own sake. Yet it also includes play with a purpose, distinguished as play (see Essay 2) because it is infused with the spirit of disinterested and poetic contemplation.

Bureaucratic thinking is primarily prescriptive or pragmatic—what I will call tinkering. There are important exceptions. By prescription, I'm referring to prescribing systems, practices, procedures, and other arrangements—prescribing what should be the case in bureaucratic systems. Tinkering is a less flattering word. By tinkering, I mean activities such as applying to a particular case a recipe selected from a repertoire of recipes.

I don't denigrate tinkering. For many years, I too was an administrative tinker person. There are different levels of tinkering; and the more superficial and the smaller the problem, the more valuable is pure tinkering. I should say that there's tiny tinkering and grand tinkering. There's the tinkering that's the work of the plumber and the tinkering that is part of the work of the physician. The plumber with his toolbox and physician with his stethoscope tinker, respectively, with the relative complexities of my house pipes and my body parts—at different levels. My point is that some tinkering is incredibly complex.

Tinkering is legitimate within bureaucratic practice; so is play. Certainly, so is science. Yet two points should be added. First, tinkering should not be considered *the* pattern, *the* model, *the* ideal, *the* form, for all levels and kinds of bureaucratic practice.

Second, thinking or theorizing should not be misconceived as subservient to an ethic of prescription—or an ethic of tinkering. The more long-term the issues, for instance, the less desirable are the prescriptive and tinkering approaches. A contrast can be drawn between macro and micro administrative issues, and I claim that disinterested contemplation is more obviously required for the former, more neglected category. A comparison I have often made for administrative thinking is between macroeconomics and microeconomics. The former deals with issues that affect the entire economy, like the employment and inflation levels. The latter deals with issues that concern the individual firm, even though that firm might be enormous (e.g., the size of General Electric or Wal-Mart).

Play can be ridiculed as ignoring day-to-day and ongoing pains and problems of others' lives. Yet such ridiculing disguises the fact that tinkering has a proven record of impotence in addressing the more fundamental issues. Both play and tinkering are unfortunate if they do not relate—not necessarily in the short run and not necessarily directly—to the kind of issues that Derrida listed as out-of-joint in the world, and tinkering should not be an excuse for ignoring them. They included massive exclusion of homeless citizens from participation in the democratic life of states; ruthless economic war between countries; inability to master contradictions in the concepts, norms, and realities of the free market; aggravation of the foreign debt; the arms industry and trade; the spread of nuclear weapons, now uncontrollable; interethnic wars; the growing power of phantom states like the mafia; and the present state of international law. This list could be extended to include, for instance, terrorism, the exploitation of women, the ecological destruction of nonrenewable resources, drug addiction, the escalating population level, and so on. All bureaucratic attempts to resolve such issues can be expected to fall victim to the dead hand.

False Prescription

That bureaucratic thinking is primarily tinkering is only half the story, however. For long, many have tinkered in practice but have nurtured a dream of establishing a science of administration. I should qualify this statement by adding that also many have conducted hermeneutic studies while wishing to escape to a happy upland of positivist truth. They dream of positivist truths that can explain the causes of bureaucratic things—and thus can prescribe practices and behaviors.

I should repeat that I am not opposed to science, properly understood. A scientific study to establish the extent of corruption in public and private enterprise is valuable, for instance. There is much else.

The dream of establishing a reputable *science* of administration perhaps is not as insistent now as it was when Luther Gulick and Lyndall Urwick published their *Papers on the Science of Administration* (1937) or when Herbert Simon wrote his *Administrative Behavior: A Study of Decision-Making Processes in Administrative Organization* (1945/1976). Simon's book is a hermeneutic book that advocates positivism, I should add. But the dream is still powerful, albeit vain. The dream is to emulate physics in producing a firm and respectable body of explanatory knowledge. The dream is to earn the respect of those who look down their noses at the floundering and the narrowness of traditional administrative studies.

Enter the rest of the disciplines and fields. The dream of emulating physics is shared by mainstream economics and behaviorist psychology. There is a powerful and disconcerting pecking order. Fields like public administration can be looked down upon by political scientists, who can be looked down upon by economists, who can be looked down upon by physicists, who are admired and envied not only for their spectacular achievements but also for their positivism.

All of this encounters the widely discussed epistemological limits of positivism, the epistemological difficulties of any scientific social science, and the difficulties of the proof of the pudding. These are issues discussed in a massive set of literatures; and, like many others, I have discussed aspects elsewhere (e.g., 1995). Even the briefest comments should begin by saying that positivism is a great conundrum. On the one hand, positivism has yielded enormous benefits; it has been a sword of liberty in constraining ignorance. On the other hand, it has been an instrument itself of pain and exclusion. Recall Foucault (1977a). There is exclusion in shaping the said and the unsaid.

A limit in positivism is the need to exclude the normative, meaning, and understanding. Positivism yields explanation rather than understanding, as just noted; it aims to identify causes rather than reasons. It doesn't deal in meaning, and it has nothing to say about the ethical. On the contrary, post-traditional play focuses on ethics, meanings, and understandings.

A second difficulty is that there is no consensus in philosophy of science about the nature of a scientific proposition, as suggested by the history of the topic through, for example, Karl Popper, Thomas Kuhn, Imre Lakatos, Paul Feyerabend, Willard-Quine, and others. Even a Popperian view of science—that it consists of propositions that have not yet been proven to be untrue—is undermined by others on this list. There is a lack of consensus in philosophy of science thinking about the nature of scientific method (see Diesing, 1991), with the principal competitors being neo-Kantian constructivism, scientific realism, and postpositivist empiricism (Boyd, 1993). So, Wisdom (1987) can write that "hardly anyone in this scientific age knows what the nature of science is. . . ." Such epistemological difficulties are acute for bureaucratic studies, as for any social science.

Now to the nonproof of the pudding! The breadth of positivist facts about bureaucratic concerns is so restricted that the resulting body of knowledge is puny when it comes to addressing any major issue of significance, like the dead hand of bureaucracy. Putting aside one trivial example in political science, no meaningful laws have ever been identified in the social sciences. Laws-in-name-only have been issued in economic theory, like the law of diminishing marginal utility; they are not like laws in physics. No law has been discovered in the administrative sciences, and I don't think that any ever will.

> Perhaps the imagination is on the verge of recovering its rights. . . . We are still living under the reign of logic, but the logical processes of our time apply only to the solution of problems of secondary interest.
>
> —*André Breton*

Suggestion #1: Imagine Poetic Contemplation as the Standard

Like play, poetry betokens for many a fluffy ornamentality that stands against the appearance of earnestness that is sought in bureaucracy: often it is misidentified with unreality. Let's recognize that there is much that is silly in poetry, in the inspired-ecstatic and in the imagination—just as there is much that is silly in rationality and in philosophy. Let's face it; there is much that is silly in governance itself. Silly stuff is not intended—of any kind.

Start by reflecting on imaginative contemplation as the wildflower planted among the wheat of governance pondering.

The Wildflower

Consider the strong reader or the strong chess player. Those who contemplate attend to meanings that are hidden. A strong reader sees creatively below surface meanings and reaches understandings that even the author may not have consciously intended. She creates meaning in the sense that, in deconstructing Rousseau's texts, Jacques Derrida the strong reader can identify meanings that escaped even Rousseau the author. The strong chess player attends with her conscious and unconscious mind to the position she is contemplating. A Bobby Fischer, a world chess champion who wanted to crush his opponents as if they were Ping-Pong balls, could sense with huge sensitivity beyond surface meanings in a position and reach understanding of deeper and subtler possibilities. There was openness, attentiveness.

The voice of contemplation is the voice of poetry. Oakeshott makes this claim as part of his account of what he calls the *conversation of mankind* and the *truancy of poetry*. He explains that this conversation of mankind began in the primeval forests. The conversation is still ongoing, with multiple voices and idioms. For him, it has as its preeminent voice what he understands as poetry, and it flourishes most mightily when it is not dominated by yells for techniques and cries for proven facts. Writes Oakeshott (1991, 490), "As civilized human beings, we are the inheritors, neither of an inquiry about ourselves and the world, nor an accumulating body of information, but of a conversation, begun in the primal forests and extended and made more articulate in the course of centuries."

I think it is a blemish to hint at "a" single conversation, although Oakeshott (1991, 491) qualifies the blemish by speaking of the conversation of mankind as "the meeting place of various modes of imagining; and in this conversation there is, therefore, no voice without an idiom of its own . . ." He writes that in this conversation "the participants are not engaged in an inquiry or a debate; there is no 'truth' to be discovered, no proposition to be proved, no conclusion sought. . . . Thoughts of different species take wing and play around one another, responding to each other's movements and provoking one another to fresh exertion" (Oakeshott, 1991, 489). The conversation of mankind is not an onward-and-upward growth of certainties, not an ascending series of hard facts. As the term implies, first and foremost it should be a conversation. Oakeshott's point is to emphasize poetry. Poetry in the context of the conversation of mankind is understood in a catholic sense as involved in writing, painting, sculpting, composing music, acting, dancing, singing, and—if he had thought of it—even thinking about bureaucracy or governance. For Oakeshott, this poetry emerges in contemplative imagining. Oakeshott tells us, as said before, that the "voice of contemplation is the voice of poetry . . . and it has no other utterance" (Oakeshott, 1991, 516).

To return to the Oakeshott "wildflower" quote given above, this kind of poetry is contemplation that will not attend to the established rules—a sort of truancy. It is contemplation that is unregimented, untamed, unshackled. It is so indifferent to anything but its own musing that it has no concern about digressing, leading to plays within a play and to dreams within the dream of life. It is contemplation that is wildly out of place, and yet the being out of place contributes richly to the place. This wildness transforms the conversation—a wildflower planted among our wheat.

An Ancient Gulf

Imaginative or poetic contemplation should encompass a bridging between the poetic and the rationalistic. The strong reader and the strong chess player both need this bridging in order to understand more deeply. So does the strong thinker about bureaucracy and governance.

> I don't question that social science analyses are important, but still, if you want to get a broad view and a long view you read a novel rather than a social science.
>
> —Leo Strauss

Contemplation should span the space on both sides of the so-called ancient war between poetry and philosophy. It was Plato of *The Republic* who wrote of this ancient war. The tragedy of the ancient war is loss of meaning, for example, loss of the broad and long view, that Leo Strauss found more in a novel than in a social science. Georgio Agamben explains this loss of understanding in his comments on the war. He writes that, "The split between poetry and philosophy testifies to the impossibility, for Western Culture, of fully possessing the object of knowledge. . . . In our culture, knowledge (according to an antimony that Aby Warburg diagnosed as the 'schizophrenia' of Western culture) is divided between inspired-ecstatic and rational-conscious poles, neither ever succeeding in wholly reducing the other" (Agamben, 1993, xvii).

It's not that the split between poetry and philosophy has never been bridged; but the bridging has been fitful at best. Passages from the more philosophic of poets, and the more poetic of philosophers, touch both sides of the divide. There is Kahlil Gibran, as one example; "We live only to discover beauty. All else is a form of waiting" (Gibran, 1995). Ironically, for another example there's Plato. In his *Symposium*, poetry and philosophy touch fingers sublimely.

Suggestion #2: Start with Plato

> The society we have described can never grow into a reality . . . till philosophers become rulers in this world, or till those we now call kings and rulers really and truly become philosophers. . . .
>
> —*Plato*

An open thinker is one who contemplates constitutive patterns, almost like Plato's philosopher-king. The term "king" is quaint. By philosopher-king, Plato meant either a ruler or an *adviser* to a ruler. We can translate king as president, prime minister, CEO, or administrator.

Both the open practitioner and Plato's ideal adviser (and ruler) contemplate constitutive patterns, although the patterns in Plato's case are far, far more fundamental. For Plato, philosophers—as in philosopher-administrators—were not narrow specialists, usually academic. Not to overromanticize them, but philosophers were wisdom lovers, who contemplated and sought to know the constitutive patterns, that is, the paradigms or models that shape the world. In the theory that he taught during his middle period, Plato described these patterns as Forms, unchanging and truly real, independently existing. He held that all items in our world-of-becoming have their qualities by participating or sharing in these Forms, which he thinks can be understood only by the mind. We need not buy into Plato's two-world view (Aristotle did not, for instance) or even understand the theory of the Forms, and it is said that he himself did not hold the theory in the beginning and the final phases of his career. But notice that Plato's philosopher-ruler, like the thinker as player, is one who contemplates constitutive patterns.

Plato would insist that contemplation requires a right relationship both to practice and to constitutive patterns; it requires both proximity and distance. His philosopher-king trainees spent fifteen years in a sort of intern capacity, and they spent fifteen years in study after completion of their general education and military/physical training. In a parallel fashion, imaginative contemplation requires not only a familiarity with what counts as common sense in bureaucratic action but also a certain freedom or distance from what-counts-as-wisdom in the active life. I suppose all this is obvious, and obviously contained, within the notion of a truancy of poetry—a wildflower planted among our wheat. Yet we should go beyond Plato.

Indignant would be his objection to the suggestion of the contemplation of *imaginative* possibilities. *The Republic,* the most famous of his twenty dialogues, celebrates the contemplation of really real patterns. It also describes an undemocratic system. It does so in the form of mind play about an ideal city that exists only in the republic of letters; it's thinking as playing.

> I want you to go on to picture the enlightenment
> or ignorance of your human condition somewhat
> as follows. Imagine an underground chamber
> like a cave. . . .
>
> —*Plato*

Going beyond Plato, we could tinker with the most celebrated metaphor in *The Republic.* We could interpret—or misinterpret—Plato's metaphor as expressing what thinking as playing hopes to achieve. Through poetic contemplation that starts with constitutive patterns of imaginative possibilities, play is trying to liberate thinkers from undue confinement to the shadows on their wall. As everyone knows, the Allegory of the Cave—beautiful in some ways, violent in others—describes prisoners chained since childhood in a cave. They are chained in such a way that they can see only a wall, on which are cast shadows of various objects by light from a fire (written in the days before movies, television, and computers!). Naturally enough, they suppose that the shadows they see are real. Then one prisoner is unchained and dragged out of the cave. He wants to stay facing the wall and to see the shadows, which are familiar and which he understands. Taken outside the cave, he is at first bedazzled and even more frightened. I will not finish the allegory. But I'll add that eventually the unchained prisoner gets used to seeing really real objects. Through poetic contemplation, so too is the aim of thinking as playing. Writes Plato (506b), "The thing he would be able to do last would be to look directly at the sun itself, and gaze at it without using reflection in water or any other medium, but as it is in itself."

2 • More Play: Like a Gadfly?

Thinkers as players with a purpose should be gadflies, as long as that includes the spirit of disinterested and poetic contemplation. A first ideal in a gadfly mission should be privileging broad-brush governance concerns, with a consequent need to match topics with new turf. A second ideal in a gadfly mission is the inclusion of voices that are excluded from, or pushed to the margins in, traditional discussions about governance.

> After all, the cultivated person's first duty is to be
> always prepared to re-write the encyclopedia.
>
> —*Umberto Eco*

A gadfly is more than a horsefly that annoys livestock. Applied to people, *gadfly* can mean a person who acts as a goad or provocative stimulus. It can mean an in-your-face critic, persistent and irritating, stirring the pot. Going beyond Plato (backward in time), Socrates was executed for charges stemming from his gadfly mission. The character Socrates in Plato's dialogue states, "It is literally true, even if it sounds rather comical, that God has specially appointed me to this city, as though it were a large thorough-bred horse which because of its great size is inclined to be lazy and needs the stimulation of some stinging fly. It seems to me that God has attached me to this city to perform the office of such a fly. . . ." (Plato, 30e). Socrates believed that, as a gadfly, he was best serving his city by his biting questioning.

Thinkers as players-with-a-purpose should be gadflies. Yet it is more than merely inflicting stings on the status quo. Gadflies are optimally effective for society when infused with, like Socrates, the spirit of disinterested and poetic contemplation. They cannot be successful in the longer run without inclusion of the spirit of the play-with-no-purpose discussed in Essay 1.

There is no system for play, however. Playfulness includes openness to all kinds of play. It has the space for play that switches gears, for play that shuffles in and out of play, for play that ambles at whim to science to hermeneutics to pragmatism and back to play. It is ready to move back and forth from poetry to crankcase oil. It has license to shift from the sublime to the banal, and hopefully back to the beautiful.

I sketch the gadfly mission in the first part of this essay. The second part discusses the ideal in a gadfly mission of privileging broad-brush governance concerns and the need to match more productive topics with new turf. The third part speaks of a second ideal in a gadfly mission, and this is the inclusion of voices that are excluded from or pushed to the margins in traditional discussions about governance.

Gadfly with an Attitude

Example #1: The supply is large of studies that can serve as cata-lysts in challenging misconceptions about the economy. There is Doug Henwood's critique of the ebullient characterization of a New Economy, for example, and it is a critique that leads naturally to questions about the relationship of such ebullience to the nature of individuals and society. Henwood describes the New Economy discourse that reached a fever pitch from 1996 to 2001 when the economic bubble popped. The New Economy was considered "the wonder of the world. Computers had unleashed a productivity miracle, recessions were things of the past, ideas had replaced things as the motors of economic life, the world had become deeply meaningful, and mutual finds had put an end to class conflict" (Henwood, 2003, 1). Henwood characterizes such delusions as characteristic of the later stages of longer-lasting booms, and he explains that these are variations of ancient themes like techno-utopianism and a frictionless economy. His contribution is a relentless debunking of the assumptions of such a New Economy.

Gadfly questioning on misconceptions of the economy might start with other sources. For one, it could begin with the curiosity that economics is now taught in some elementary schools. States a Virginia college course catalog for Economics 400 for future elementary school teachers, "Teachers will learn how to make economics come alive in their classroom. Teachers will learn how to teach basic economics principles addressing scarcity, production, consumption, opportunity cost, markets, etc." *Why?* For another source, the questioning might begin with, say, Joseph Stiglitz's *The Roaring Nineties: A New History of the World's Most Prosperous Decade* (2003).

Example #2: On arteriosclerosis in government and in large bureaucracies, the gadfly might start with a publication like Helen Caldicott's *The New Nuclear Danger* (2002). In her sober account of a world-terminating danger, Caldicott is on a gadfly mission. Among other questions, she asks who runs government. Her answer is the

> transnational corporations whose executives wine and dine, woo, bribe, and corrupt the officeholders of the White House and Congress . . . These all-powerful corporations manipulate and control most of the federal legislation, foreign and domestic. . . . They do it through a variety of mechanisms: think tanks, corporate mergers, lobbying, and political donations. (2002, 24)

Such gadfly questioning might continue from the vast literature that is available. For example, there is Richard Clarke's *Against All Enemies: Inside America's War on Terror* (2004). This is a political critique. But it is also about governmental bureaucracy. In discussing the benefits of face-to-face meetings between agency heads, for instance, Clarke speaks of such problems as shaking information from within agencies.

A function of the gadfly is to tell the city what it does not want to know. But it is not simply a matter of biting. Needed for the longer-run benefit of society is gadfly thinking that, as mentioned, is infused with disinterested and poetic contemplation.

The gadfly aim contrasts with a role like oiling the wheels of governance. I agree that economists who forecast, political scientists who advise on election campaigns, business consultants who design company strategies, and public administration thinkers who recommend institutional changes are providing highly skilled help. So do butlers and mechanics, weather forecasters and physicians. Where the purpose is other than to gadfly, however, play with a purpose is decidedly *less* in the public interest. It is *less*, like a CEO spending time in the mailroom sorting the company mail, like an opera singer crooning popular ditties, like a physicist fixing a broken electric lamp, like a poet writing a grocery list, like a neurosurgeon peddling drug products. Lesser activities surely can be done, and they may be beneficial. But they are suboptimal for society, because to gadfly is too rare.

The character of gadfly help also shifts away from a theory-practice model that seeks to transmit ideas through the present practitioner as that job is currently constituted, especially the midlevel employee in fields like public administration. It moves toward the model of the help provided by the study of, say, macro-economics, where there is no expectation that what is learned will speak directly on Monday morning to my job as an air conditioner salesperson. Yet, a reconstituted practice as art (see Essays 13 through 18) can be a significant conduit and source.

A First Gadfly Ideal: Topic and Turf

The gadfly mission is better, for one thing, when it privileges broad-brush governance concerns. For this, it must be prepared to appropriate topic and turf. So should the play described in Essay 1.

Imagine economic and bureaucratic arrangements in a world where the Cold War's end removed competitive alternatives to capitalism! Or, imagine the arrangements in a world without advertising! Or, imagine (see Essay 13) the relationship between *the totality of political, economic, and administrative systematizing* and *the individuality of the human*. Soon I will give another example— about population trends. The gadfly mission should link society and narrow specialty, operating in both directions. Turf boundaries for such play can be tailor-made and retailed at convenience, sufficient for central attention to such larger societal topics.

This creates a personnel problem. Most specialists are amateurish outside their fields. In my own case, for instance, I will always be amateurish on hotel or sports administration, despite any reading I might do. The challenge is that specialists should be prepared (and they should prepare themselves, as discussed in Essay 4) to emerge from their subject-matter redoubts, risking appearing amateurish.

Dual Directionality

The gadfly can direct her thinking inward toward affecting administrative, economic, political, or other practice. But a second direction is inside out to generate insights about society and human life, that is, about the nonadministrative, noneconomic, or nonpolitical. In other words, the street is two-directional.

> By the middle of this century, the United States will no longer be a majority non-Hispanic white nation—and the very concept and meaning of race will have evolved.
>
> —*The Ninety-Eighth American Assembly*

The American Assembly (2001), in its report on race relations, serves to illustrate this dual directionality. Its understandings about society are directed inward toward insights about political, administrative, and economic institutions and practices. The American Assembly (2001, 4) recommends that the "Immigration and Naturalization Service should [emphasize] . . . incorporating new immigrants into society" and that "metropolitan regions must be willing to undertake the difficult tasks of increasing linkages between cities and suburbs." Yet also, gadfly thinking can be directed outward toward insights on the social construction of racial conditions. The American Assembly suggests that by midcentury "the very concept and meaning of race will have evolved." Shouldn't governance thinkers join with scholars who have already conducted studies on how institutions and policies shape society and human life? As another example for dual directionality, I can reflect on society in order to goad police arrangements. Also, from contemplating the police cauldron, I can seek insights about society and human life.

Tailored Scope

The scope required for thinking as a gadfly is broader than is available in a single truncated discourse like political science, economics, or the administrative specializations—public administration, business administration, hotel administration, sports administration, travel administration, and so on. But I don't think that we need wait for disciplinary restructuring, because each of us as individuals can do what has to be done in our own way—without a permission slip. The scope at each end of the dual directionality can be tailored and retailored to suit the needs of the particular study.

Pipe Dream

The wider scope of governmentality is desirable. In an institutional way, the governmentality turf could be considered as including whatever kinds of systems and arrangements shape individuals—the larger societal topic mentioned earlier! Candidate institutions would include public and business agencies—and other agencies like churches, nonprofits, schools, and families. Earlier I suggested (1995, 118–119) that governmentality be defined in terms of publicness, including publicness in private organizations. Publicness refers to aspects of goods and services, including private goods and services, where "the benefits . . . are indivisible, and people cannot be excluded from using" them (Samuelson & Nordhaus, 1989). In the introduction I described governance widely to include ways in which political, economic, and administrative power and authority are exercised.

Yet it's a pipe dream to work toward a massive lumping together of fields and disciplines in a transdiscipline that we could call, say, heteronomics. The scope of such a heteronomics would have to extend through the subject matter turfs now cultivated by political science, economics, political economy, moral philosophy, sociology, civil society, the complex of action subjects like public administration, business administration, social work—and beyond. The ideal scope would include turfs that relate to the biological, the psychological, the social, and the spiritual. It would involve other subjects like history and literature, for example, incorporating not only the history of political ideas but also the history of economic ideas. Vertically, the ideal scope would have to extend from the most general to the most particular. It would reach from the generality of the current turfs of subjects like philosophical ethics and sociology to the patches of particularized subject matter staked out by the action subjects, like criminal justice management. A return—if it's a return—to the unity of knowledge has been a dream of many distinguished thinkers throughout the modern period, like Immanuel Kant and Auguste Comte. An obvious problem is that the reform is probably impossible; the cat's out of the bag. I don't think it is really helpful to seek such a broadening of scope *organizationally*—seeking salvation through a massive top-down structure of disciplinary reform.

Tailoring

A tailored and ad hoc approach is needed where the better model for knowing (as Deleuze & Guattari, 1987, explain) is the rhizome rather than the tree. I admire this metaphor. The rhizome is a rootlike and typically horizontal stem that grows along or under the ground, sending out roots below and stems above. In the rhizome model, understandings and explanations are decentered. Contrasted against this is the arborescent view that sees the various divisions of knowledge arranged like the branches and twigs of a tree, holding that there is an essential rootedness and unity of knowledge.

Poster boys for the tailored and retailored approach in governance thinking could be great thinkers like Herbert Marcuse and Adam Smith. An example (arbitrarily selected) could be Marcuse's *Eros and Civilization* (1955). His penetrating analysis includes materials from philosophy, psychoanalysis, politics, economics, and other disciplines. It is replete with insights, such as speaking of how mass democracy provides "the political paraphernalia" for introjecting the reality principle.

> Mass democracy . . . allows the masters to disappear behind the technological veil of the productive and destructive apparatus which they control, and it conceals the human (and material) costs of the benefits and comforts which it bestows upon those who collaborate. (Marcuse, 1955, xii–xiii)

Such thinking draws from what it needs, and it synthesizes the ideas.

A Second Gadfly Ideal: Anti-Administration

The gadfly mission is better, for a second thing, when it embraces the spirit of contemplation that includes voices excluded from, or marginalized, in traditional discussions of governance. For this, anti-administration is helpful. Anti-administration was developed for the field of public administration, and thus the name. But it applies no less to other governance disciplines and fields. A primary aim has been to encourage anti-administrative consciousness in related disciplines like political science and economics, as I have explained (Farmer, 2001, 475–492).

Example: Touch is important for humans, and yet it is a topic that is not on the agenda of traditional thinking about administration. Significant benefits for premature babies have been described for skin-to-skin (kangaroo), rather than traditional incubator, care: kangaroo care occurs when a parent holds the premature baby for a period each day (Feldman et al., 2002, 16–25). Soothing music has also been described as significant for neonatal behavioral states in hospital newborn nursing (Kaminski & Hall, 1996, 45–54.) Politicians, priests, and physicians have always known the value of touching. But in administrative settings like prisons, the topic is not recognized for the importance it must have. Here a symbol of absence of *human* touch could be some two thousand Mariel boatlift people, still incarcerated indefinitely on no charges (Town, 2004). Antisocial behavior inevitable? It gets worse; touching in bureaucracy, even in elementary school teaching, is now a legal hazard. But it is counterproductive in the long run for the gadfly mission to suppose that touch is *the* secret of better administration.

Anti-administration is a model for a kind of gadfly attitude that is desirable. Looked at from one broad perspective, an actual situation can be described in a distinctive way. Viewed from another, the same actuality can be redescribed. What is the case does not change; instead (see Essay 6), it is redescribed or re-imagined. Looking from an economic perspective, I see administrative actions that can be explained in rational and self-interested terms. Looking from some psychological perspectives, I see actions that can be explained as emanating from both the conscious and the unconscious. Looking from an ecological or sociological or spiritual or biological or linguistic perspective, I see a different description of what is. I see an *other*.

Anti-administration wants to include not only mainstream ideas but also ideas that are other. "Other" here includes, as just implied, the ideas of people who are excluded and marginalized, for example, financially poor clients and citizens, minorities and women, and employees in dealing with their bosses. "Other" also refers to ideas from discourses that are not dominant, for example, non-mainstream or alternative economics, nonmainstream administrative thinking, queer theory, ecological views. But it is more. In analyzing bureaucratic questions, for instance, there is not enough focus on the nonmechanical, the nonbureaucratic, the nonsystematic (Farmer & R.L. Farmer, 1997). Anti-administration stands against a reform program of tinkering only with parts, failing to recognize appropriately the interconnectedness of all that is.

Anti-administration implicates two impulses—the anti impulse and the pro impulse. The "anti" impulse is against limitations that discourage openness in ways of thinking and doing. It is against the dominance of assumptions embedded in mainstream concepts. The pro impulse is "for" concepts that open thinking and doing. In public administration, these are the interacting concepts of imaginization, deconstruction, deterritorialization, alterity, and reflexive language. More complete and therefore more complicated accounts are given, for instance, in my introduction to a 2001 symposium (Farmer, 2001, 475–492) and elsewhere (e.g., Farmer, 1995, 2002).

Papers by post-traditional thinkers in the 2001 symposium add significant contributions to the idea of anti-administration. O.C. McSwite (2001, 493–506) provides a rationale for anti-administration in terms of Lacanian psychoanalytic theory. McSwite suggests that anti-administration should be seen as relating to our contemporary social context, especially the commercialization of the world and the decay of the social bond. Michael Spicer (2001, 507–528) argues for value pluralism that is consistent with anti-administration, and he suggests that the monist ethical view is dangerous.

Patricia M. Patterson (2001, 529–540) illuminates the radically antibureaucratic character of anti-administration by personifying it and drawing a comparison with the trickster folk figure. She holds that anti-administration seems to contend, as many feminisms do, that the prevailing questions need reframing. Richard Box (2001, 559–572) sees a clear connection between private lives and anti-administration. He suggests a focus on public administrators exercising their imaginative faculties to protect private lives.

Robert Cunningham and Robert Schneider (2001, 573–588) discuss witnessing and gifting as anti-administrative strategies for reclaiming what they describe as a trust relationship between civil servants and citizens. They choose to express their ideas in theological language. "Witnessing and gifting involve sharing uncomfortable truths, making self vulnerable to the other by taking risks, breaking organizational norms by telling the truth, and going beyond what is normally expected in providing or refusing the service" (Cunningham & Schneider, 2001, 580). Janet Hutchinson (2001, 589–604) illustrates the relevance of an anti-administrative stance, using a feminist perspective. She holds that anti-administration is antimelancholy, and she suggests that multigendering is one remedy for what she describes as the pervasive melancholy that afflicts women, men, and organizations.

Debra Jacobs (2001, 605–620) offers an ecological argument for anti-administration, indicating how the ideas of technocratic administration exclude the ideas of deep ecologists. The most striking image in her paper, for me, is that of the cow and the highway. "Life within the machine is ordered being. Technologic being is an ordered existence, premised upon rules, hierarchical relationships and rationality. The 'chaos' of nature is the other, in this telling, because it exists in opposition to the orderliness of modernity. Imagine for an instance a cow standing in the middle of the highway as you drive to work. The chaos destabilizes your world: it does not belong there. . . . (Jacobs, 2001, 490–491). As she concludes, the "cow simply does not belong on the road."

A gadfly mission seeking the ideal of anti-administration is in the spirit of *rewriting* that Jean-Francois Lyotard discusses. Lyotard's rewriting is not an attempt to grasp the past *correctly*. It is similar to free association. Attitudes toward play include suspending judgment, being patient, and giving attention to everything that happens. It is not, as discussed in Essay 6, Big T Truth. "Contrary to remembering, working through would be defined as a work without end, and therefore without will: without end in the sense in which it is not guided by the concept of an end—and without finality" (Lyotard, 1991, 30). The gadfly mission should not imagine that it is presenting certain, complete, and absolute truth (see Essay 6). Notice that Socrates, long before Lyotard, never pretended to do that. He questioned. The gadfly mission stings better when it opens up possibilities.

3 • Self and Detritus

Thinking as playing should aim to clear space for each individual self to achieve her fullest potential. Attention is invited to the whole person-in-herself in-her-difference. It is also directed to the contested character of the self, pointing to the self as detritus of relevant language.

The coming being is whatever being.

—*Giorgio Agamben*

The main interest in life is to become someone
else that you were not at the beginning. . . .
The game is worthwhile insofar as we don't
know what we will be at the end.

—*Michel Foucault*

Post-traditional thinking, I agree, should aim to clear the space for each individual self to be all she can be. Self first, system second! Self first, institution second! The self should be privileged. Yet each of us inherits deep ignorance about the self that lives, laughs, smiles, loves, suffers, inflicts pain, dreams, and much more. The nature of the self is a contested philosophical topic.

By self, I mean—to use a slogan—the whole person-in-herself in-her-difference. It's not a person reduced to a time slice, but a whole human self. It is not a person reduced to a system appendage or function, a customer or an employee. It is not a person merely as a member of a group. It is a distinctive human individual, unreduced.

This essay is divided into five unequal parts, each of them related to an aim of governance thinking as clearing space for the individual self. The first part reminds of warnings about privileging system over self. The second discusses privileging the individual. The third part talks about the idea of a "whole person." The fourth starts to discuss the remainder of the jingle "whole person-in-herself in-her-difference." The fifth continues the discussion by commenting on the contested character of the self, pointing to the self as detritus of relevant language.

Privileging System over Self

> The great question is . . . what can we oppose to this
> machinery in order to keep a portion of mankind free
> from this parceling-out of the soul, from this supreme
> mastery of the bureaucratic way of life.
>
> —*Max Weber*

Early post-traditional thinkers like Max Weber and Herbert Marcuse are among those who write powerfully about the inhumanity of privileging systems. That is, they write about the anti-human effects of modern economic and bureaucratic systems. Weber writes of the Faustian bargain that we make with the economic-bureaucratic system. The cost is high. We trade our "full and beautiful humanity" in return for a narrow vocation where we are "specialists without spirit, sensualists without heart" in a rationalized and disenchanted world (Weber, 1958, 182). Modern capitalist culture is described by Weber as resembling an "iron cage." Care for external goods should be worn like a light cloak, but "fate decreed that the cloak should become an iron cage" (Weber, 1958, 181). Some would say that, more precisely, Weber uses the image of the steel shell (e.g., Chalcraft, 1994); they point out that Talcott Parsons should have translated *"ein stahlhartes Gehause"* as "steel shell." The economic-bureaucratic system, like a steel shell or an iron cage, exerts ever larger demands on the people who have no choice but to belong to the system. In Weber's words (1958, 181), the "tremendous cosmos of the economic order" is "now bound to the technical and economic conditions of machine production which today determine the lives of all the individuals who are born into this mechanism."

Curiously, the intentions of writers like Max Weber often have been distorted in ideologies like traditional American public administration. Weber has been misdescribed as the "inventor" of modern bureaucracy and as advocating the ideal type characteristics of modern bureaucracy (e.g., *The PA Times* 2001). If he could hear such misrepresentations, surely he would turn in his grave. On second thought, recognizing the power of ideological belief to distort contrary data, perhaps it's not curious.

Marcuse (1991) writes of one-dimensional thinking that uncritically accepts existing structures and norms. He describes two features in "the most advanced areas of industrial society." They are "a trend toward consummation of technological rationality, and intensive efforts to contain this trend within the established institutions" (Marcuse, 1991, 17). Marcuse maintains that individuals are unfree when functioning within systems like the economy. Only when free from systems are they free to determine what they really want. Subject to systems, they are limited by the range of choices presented in the economy; they have "false needs."

A symphony of thinkers has said similar things in different ways. For instance, there is Jürgen Habermas (1987) with his distinction between the life-world and that of systems.

Such post-traditional writers explain why they warn that economic and bureaucratic systems are inhumane to the extent that they privilege the nonhuman over the human. We are familiar with the fact that talk about the economy as a whole can disguise understanding about the fate of the individual in that economy, for example, the economy doing better while good jobs go overseas. But these writers go further. They speak of a denial of humanity when the human is not privileged. A malignancy exists in governance thinking that does not take the self as its first concern.

Privileging Self over System

Amina Lawal had been sentenced to death by stoning for adultery. In September 2003 the Islamic appeals court in Nigeria threw out the absurd death sentence on Lawal. The triumph was declared a group or system triumph, not merely a victory for the individual.

The appeals panel gave group or system reasons for overturning the sentence. The system required, for example, that persons can be guilty only if caught in the act of adulterous sex. She was not in that group, and the system was not interested in the apparent fact that she had given birth to an illegitimate baby. It's an example where the system, the group, was vindicated. As the defense attorney exulted, "It's a victory for law. It's a victory for justice."

There can be tension between the group-think of official administration and the individual-think of a street administrator. Tension can be relieved between group and individual, for example, when a functionary like a police officer acts in recognition of the individual circumstances that prompt treatment contrary to official "group" laws, systems, policies, and procedures. Yet the fact remains that governance typically relates to groups of people. Typically it relates to individuals insofar as they are members of specific groups.

Public and private agencies continue to delineate the individual person in group terms, appendages to agency needs. Aiming for efficiency in provisioning, the agency and the corporation conceptualize employees, customers, and clients all as those who *exist for.* The employee as a unit of thinking is one who "exists for" the purposes of the agency or corporation. More controversially, even the customer or client is reduced to a part in that he is considered only insofar as he is to be serviced by the agency. Even when it speaks of "existing for" the customer, the agency has an operational notion of a customer limited to one "existing for" the service from the agency. Economic man, administrative man, and political man; as mentioned in Essays 15 and 17, they are units of analysis that "exist for."

Existing for can be understood better by reflecting on Immanuel Kant's categorical imperative. Distinguishing between persons as means and persons as ends, the categorical imperative provides that a person should not be treated as a means *only.* Customers or clients of an economic or political system are not fully human; they are not ends. They are not humans, unreduced. For the economic system, customers exist for the benefits of the larger economic sys-

tem and for the products offered by a particular firm. Customers of
a roof repair company can exist merely for buying roof repairs, for
instance. For the political system, clients or customers exist for the
benefits of the governmental service. So, clients of a department of
taxation (or of transportation) exist for the purpose of paying their
taxes (or using transportation). Try applying Kant's imperative on
your next visit to the dry cleaners, treating the sales clerk as an end
and not as a means only. Then, try it on a client. That can reinforce
a feeling of the meaning of *existing for.*

"Why, in the context of terrorism, should the needs of the state
be privileged above the rights of victims?" asks Jennifer Short
(2004). She is referring to the legal activity of Ron Motley, who is
legal counsel for some individual victims in suing certain Saudi
individuals for the September 11 attacks. She is contrasting the
needs of the individual with those of the system. Without making
judgment, I mention this case to continue to open up the matter of
clearing space for human individuals to achieve their fullest potential. It is a clearing of space even against the wants of the system that presumably has a wish to maintain relations between the
United States and Saudi Arabia. Motley is described as reversing
the treatment of this historical event of terrorism as being primarily of group, rather than of individual, interest.

Clearing space for individual humans to achieve their fullest
potential can be described in various ways. In the language of
Matthew Arnold in nineteenth-century England, I suppose it might
be expressed as each and every man [*sic*] being treated as if he
were a Christian gentleman; in a language familiar in the United
States, each and every person is treated as if rich and well connected. In the slogan I prefer, post-traditional thinking should focus on directing governance toward each *whole person-in-herself
in-her-difference* achieving her fullest potential. Each and every
person should be treated not only as a whole but also in terms of
each of his or her dimensions of being human. Essay 9 writes of
human dimensions as the biological, the social, the psychological,
the moral, the spiritual, and other aspects of the human person.
The parameters for treating persons will be determined by political and other decisions. For example, political masters may deter-

mine that only a few (e.g., the rich) should be treated as entitled. In that case, it could be the task of the practitioner to work within the political and legal constraints toward the larger aim. The governance thinker would have a free hand, nevertheless—including that of critic and commentator.

The post-traditional consciousness of privileging self over system stands against a view of governance as a set of subject matter fields that, although giving strong lip service to people, focuses in practice primarily on institutions. It stands against thinking that in practice is engrossed in managing and maintaining bureaucratic, economic, and other systems. Fascination with the self qua self has danced around the edges of traditional efforts to reduce bureaucratic and economic understandings to matters of the mere efficiency of systems.

Post-traditional thinking can oppose governance that gives primary attention to groups and subgroups of people. Thus such thinking as playing can turn attention to governmentality. Michel Foucault writes of governmentality not only as the government of nation-states but also as individual self-government. He describes self-government in terms of technologies of the self—the ways in which I am shaped and the ways in which I rule myself. Recall Foucault's 1979–80 course outline. It speaks of governmentality as "understood in the wider sense of techniques and procedures designed to direct the behavior of men [sic]. Government of children, government of souls or consciences, government of a household, of the State or of oneself" (Carrette, 2000, 133).

The proper study of human systems is the individual self, not the system as an end in itself. Each way of describing the privileging of self over system lacks force, however, without exploring the idea of the whole person-in-herself in-her-difference. The latter includes considering the contested nature of the self.

A Whole Person

And one man in his time plays many parts,
His acts being seven ages. At first the infant,
Mewling and puking in his nurse's arms.
And then the whining school-boy, . . .

> . . . . Last scene of all,
> That ends this strange eventful history,
> Is second childishness and mere oblivion,
> Sans teeth, sans eyes, sans taste, sans everything.

Shakespeare writes of the seven ages of "one man" (*As You Like It,* II, vii, 139). The seven ages, or stages, start with the infant. It proceeds through the stage of the whining schoolboy "creeping like a snail" to school; the lover "sighing like a furnace"; the soldier "full of strange oaths" and "seeking the bubble reputation"; the justice with a "round belly"; and the aging man with "shrunk shank." It ends with the man in his second childhood—without teeth, without eyes, without taste, without everything.

Marvelous it is to walk and talk with any eight or nine-year-old! Each is a miracle, full of life, huge possibilities, and outpouring imaginative energy. Unless stricken down by some quirk of ill fate, each individual child will have a whole life in the sense that s/he will proceed through a set of stages similar to the ones that Shakespeare describes. The stages will exhibit radical diversity, as female and male are involved—and as various cultures and ethnicities are constitutive. Philosophers have disagreed about personal identity, and it is difficult to put one's finger on what it is that persists through a person's radical changes. Consider the well-known example of Theseus's wooden boat that rots and where each and every plank is eventually replaced. At which point, if any, in the transferring of planks does the boat cease to be the same boat? Similarly, if my body parts were sequentially replaced by cyberparts, at what point—if any—would I become a cyborg? Yes, each eight or nine-year-old may change so that s/he becomes virtually unrecognizable as the once little infant. S/he may forget her/his infancy completely. Doesn't s/he persist as the same living person, however we account for it? I think so. The ages (stages) can be analyzed, and enjoyed; but no stage is actually detachable. In brief, s/he is a whole living being.

Political and economic systems—policies and administration—typically treat persons as less than fully whole living beings. (As suggested, also they typically treat groups rather than Shakespeare's

SELF AND DETRITUS 39

"one man.") Political policy-making in traditional government systematically creates systems that deal with discrete time slices of groups in the population, and the individuals benefited or affected become time slices. The U.S. welfare program provides one example. The welfare recipient is a category limited to the slices of time when the category applies. The recipient hauls herself from one program office to another during the times when she falls into particular subcategories. She treks from one place to another, for example, from this food stamp appointment here to that Medicaid appointment there. A program for persons with schizophrenia, for instance, recognizes only two kinds of persons—those with, and those without, schizophrenia, receiving the benefits of the prescribed amounts for the prescribed time slices. The men of system can well argue that this is efficient; the reason they can say this is the lack of a better theory.

Economic corporations and companies treat employees as time-sliced groups. In this, it follows mainstream economic theory. Labor is one of the four factors of production—land, labor, capital, and organizing ability; and the same comments could be offered about the other human factor. Labor is treated as a unit over a period of time and not as a person with a whole life. When they are hired and fired, my grandchildren will not be regarded as persons who were born and who must proceed in a connected way through life until they are "sans teeth, sans eyes, sans taste, sans everything." Little David and little Tyler will not be David and Tyler. For specified segments of time they will be regarded as units of labor at time t1, unless they are lucky enough to manage a corporation—in which case they will be "units of organizing ability at time t1." In a theory conceived in modernity, the economic theorizing approach has always been oddly "postmodern" in treating people as if they were disjointed bits. Again, the economic practitioner will ask what he can do; he can well point his finger of blame at the theorist.

Person-in-Herself In-Her-Difference

The subtlety and complexity of a person-in-herself in-her-difference presents intensifying challenges for governance. It is a subtlety that Jacques Derrida intended to symbolize in playing on the fact that the difference between the French words *différance* and *différence* is inaudible. There is complexity in the democratization of individual difference.

Democratization of difference is a label for a context where individual differences primarily are those that count rather than a context where group differences are primary. There should be a shift toward democratization of difference, and discussion of this shift toward democratization can be started in such terms as direction.

"Locke was the son of a country lawyer." This is how a very respectable scholarly book (its name and author escape me) starts to summarize John Locke. The philosopher Locke is being characterized by his source, although we know that more important is what he became. This illustrates a tendency that we have inherited to speak of a person in terms of her origins. It is a reasonable tendency, as most psychoanalysts will agree. But there is another even more reasonable direction, and this looks forward to what the person will become. The point about the future is that, in the middle of his life, Locke did not know what he would become. There is an unknown emphasis in the future direction.

Homi Bhabha, Giorgio Agamben, and Michel Foucault (see quotes at the head of this essay) speak to this future direction. But an emphasis on futurity is not merely a modern idea. A Greek notion, shared by Aristotle, is that the quality of a life cannot properly be assessed until the person is dead. The person just does not know how her life will turn out.

The person-in-herself in-her-difference in this context is explained better by Homi Bhabha than by Giorgio Agamben. Bhabha gives a picture of the self as constituting her future within the web of the opportunities and constraints afforded by society. This web that creates or cocreates the self is the language specifying the way(s) of looking at the self and at the self's functioning in the world. Agamben is less useful if he is seen as saying that the self can be anything. Yet it is valuable if he is read as saying that the self, not limited to a particular description, is open to a multitude of possibilities.

Bhabha contributes to postcolonial theory in writing that the "interstitial passage between fixed identifications opens up the possibility of cultural hybridity that entertains difference without an assumed or imposed hierarchy" (Bhabha, 1994, 4). His work includes a focus on those moments or processes that are produced in the articulation of cultural differences. These "in-between spaces provide the terrain of elaborating strategies of selfhood—singular or communal—that initiate new signs of identity, and innovative site of collaboration and contestation, in the act of defining the idea of society itself."

A few years ago one of my garden fences blew down. Rather than buy a new one, I propped up the broken fence by using a piece of rope to tie it to a drainpipe on the house. The result was precarious, in present danger of collapse. To my amazement, a spider spun a large and elaborate web affixed to the rope and the broken fence. I wanted to warn the spider; but I was limited to admiring her elegance. It's in such interstices (play Samuel Barber's *Adagio for Strings!*) that the selves described by Bhabha are created.

Agamben tells us that the person is "whatever being." He explains that this "whatever being" is not designated by a property but only by her being. Of this "whatever being," Agamben (1993a, 1) writes that "whatever" relates to "singularity not in its indifference with respect to a common property . . . but only in its being as such." He goes on to explain that "Whatever singularity has no identity, it is not determinate with respect to a concept, but neither is it simply indeterminate; rather it is determined only through a relation to an idea, that is, to the totality of its possibilities" (Agamben, 1993a, 67).

Agamben is asking us to look forward to a person being fulfilled, without being a member. It is hard to envision social arrangements other than those we have long known; for instance, it is not easy to understand how the concept of "nation-state" could have been absent in, say, twelfth-century Europe. Many find it difficult to appreciate how we could think about someone like (say) an Italian (or a man), and not color our thinking with the idea that that is an Italian (or a man). Many find it hard to think/feel that that person could just be a person, without being subject to the discourse of what it is to be a man (or an Italian). Giorgio is Giorgio, sans classification by group membership; he is also whoever he is, without the name. Giorgio is also a self to be defined in the future.

There always has been individual difference; but now this is being increasingly extended from the relatively few to the relatively many. Our grandchildren and their human relationships are being (re)constructed by political and socioeconomic rip tides, such as the decline in significance of the nation-state, the accelerating effects of communications and other technology, and massive migrations. Personal relations are being socially reconstructed by the powerful undermining of the central Enlightenment rationalizing idea that constituted the modernist era; greater rationalization means more and more happiness and moral behavior (Habermas, 1983). Undermining rationalization have been developments as old as Freudianism (see Essay 6) and as recent as the collection of views described by general terms like postmodernism.

I am less interested in whether there has been a shift than that there *should* be such a movement toward democratization of difference. The melting pot attitude that contemplates that an immigrant will give up the idiosyncrasies of the old country and emerge homogenized as an American symbolizes a resolution of group differences. The pot symbolizes groups, hyphenated groups. An individual-focused level of difference, much to be preferred, abandons all talk of pots.

We are used to the complexity of group differences and to variations within groups. So we are not too surprised, even in a society where it is said that one cannot be either too rich or too thin, to read that in a distant and radically different society like Mauritania some young Arab girls are force-fed so that they become hugely fat and therefore more desirable for marriage and libidinal purposes (Harter, 2004). We are not surprised that many people in the American South are still worried about the Civil War and that they have a strong admiration for things military, while others in other regions are not. We are prepared for the fact that environments vary and that individuals as group members are socially constructed; cultures and subcultures vary, yielding different groups of persons.

Adjusting to radical individual difference, not to be explained primarily by groups, is harder. The man with the pin-striped suit stands next to his neighbor whose forehead is covered with tattoos and whose face sports two nails sticking out from under his lower lip. The devoted churchgoer lives next to the equally devoted atheist neighbor. But the plot thickens when we come to detritus.

Detritus

It is unclear what the self is, and it is not even clear that a unitary concept of the self is viable. Enter detritus. By *detritus,* I mean the figurative equivalent of loose grains that result from the disintegration of rocks. For my money, the self is what is constituted as a kind of detritus of a language of the self.

Notice two conflicting languages or pictures of the self, one stable and the other not. Given prominence by René Descartes and the Enlightenment is the language of the centered self as a self-contained, self-mastering individual, providing a firm foundation for certainty in knowing. Stability and reliability exude. A post-traditional view is the language of the decentered self as constituted in sites like race, class, gender, culture, and power. It includes the idea of a fleeting self that is in flux, in fragments, and in dislocation. This decentered view is based on a mixture of psychoanalytic discourse and poststructural thinking. For a view that the concept of the unitary self is not coherent, notice the picture of the dialogical self (Hermans & Kempen, 1993). This speaks of the self as multiple selves in dialogue, as a nonunitary embodiment that transcends individualism and rationalism. For the claim that the unitary self is undesirable, see Deleuze and Guattari (1977). They celebrate (using "schizophrenic" in their own sense) a revolutionary schizophrenic self. They embrace multiplicity, discontinuity, and nonlinearity in the constitution of self.

The decentered picture, represented in the formula whole person-in-herself in-her-difference, invites attention first toward the language that constitutes the self. As Heidegger explains, "Human beings remain committed to and within the being of language, and can never step out of it and look at it from somewhere else" (Heidegger, 1971, 134). But I'm making the language of the self appear too orderly. There are languages or discourses, packed upon languages that are packed upon other languages. For example, the language of being a woman may be affixed to the language of being a Southerner, which may be attached to the language of being an American, which may be related to the language of being a modernist, and so on. It is a picture that displaces any simple— repeat simple—turn toward the inner world of the self.

Logically, language is prior to the individual human self, if it is not possible to be a human self without a relevant language. At first sight, this might seem unhelpful to governance. At second sight, it opens a range of imaginative possibilities for thinking as playing. Foucault recommends some of them. His recommendations include recognizing that the "group must not be the organic bond uniting hierarchized individuals, but a constant generator of de-individualization" (Foucault, 1977, xiii–xiv). Foucault implies that we should attend to the relevant language.

4 • Writing, with a Deviant Signature

All thinkers are institutionalized; the question is what to do about it. I recommend that post-traditional thinkers should be conscious about both individual and group signatures. I favor recognizing links between what is written and the life of the thinker. I suggest starting from the edge of the group's paradigm or from the in-between space between paradigms.

Write yourself! Writing is for you, you are for you; your body is yours, take it.

—*Hélène Cixous*

Information is endlessly available to us; where shall wisdom be found?

—*Harold Bloom*

Baruch Spinoza was offered in his later years a professorship at the University of Heidelberg. He declined the offer because he thought that such institutional employment would crimp his ability to philosophize independently. He continued to grind lenses for a living and to philosophize, and his death from phthisis probably resulted from the dust of his lens-grinding. On the matter of institutions, he was right.

Institutional employees are institutionalized. Working for a government, a company, or a university tends to institutionalize understanding and reasoning. Some employees are affected more than others, and relatively few not at all. At one level institutionalization makes thinking unduly sensitive to that institution's perspective. At another level it bends thinking toward that perspective. At yet another level the institution virtually owns the individual's writing, thinking. This is agreeable for some affected employees because the institution can reward by granting monies, promotion, and even a corner office; the institution can also punish. Yet it's more complicated, in two ways.

The first complication is that there are visible and invisible institutions, and both kinds of institutionalization can warp writing and thinking to a greater or lesser degree. For those in visible institutions, the chains are visible. Yet those outside institutions can be no less institutionalized, although the latter are entangled in what (adapting Karl Marx) we can call invisible chains. Visible institutions are more than employing agencies. They include professional and other traditions to which a person subscribes, for example, a physician's perspective being shaped by the traditional body of medical practice. Invisible institutionalization occurs in the form of other memberships, like nationality, region, class, and language. It occurs in terms of one's time period in history, for example, Thomas Aquinas could not have written in the same way as John Stuart Mill. My writing is helped as well as hindered, liberated as well as chained, by multiple group-paradigms, multiple group signatures.

The second complication is that not all locations within a paradigm, within an institution, are equally limiting. In other words, the group signature is not uniformly restrictive, nor uniformly liberating. The spaces toward the edges seem freer, two standard deviations away being better than one. Even less restrictive is the space between group signatures, between disciplines.

In the first part of this essay, I suggest that thinking as playing should rely on an individual signature that links what is written with the writer's lived experience. In the second part, I suggest that the thinker as player should seek to become oriented toward the edge of the group's paradigm. Better still, she should learn a second paradigm so that she can enter the space between paradigms.

Individual Signature

"Write yourself! Writing is for you, you are for you; your body is yours, take it," urges Hélène Cixous. She wants me (and you) to write with an individual signature, my (your) symbolic marking as when I (you) sign my (your) individual signature in a distinctive way. It emanates from my humanity, my body, my lived experiences.

First Person Writing

This is the "feminine writing" that Hélène Cixous (1980) advocates. This writing, somatic writing or thinking, is not reserved for women. Cixous's view is that some women are bad at feminine writing, and some men are good at it. Feminine writing, in her view, involves "a transformation of our relationship to our body (and to another body)" (Cixous, 1980, 97). It entails what can be called *writing with my body.* To mis-summarize it as a slogan, I would describe feminine writing, like somatic writing, as writing from within my guts, from within my lived experience.

Somatic writing seeks to be unbridled. It is an outpouring of the inner self or libidinal energy as the play of writing is engaged. For Cixous, it is life-affirming. Rightly, it wants to be independent of what she calls the oppression of the phallologocentric. Writes Cixous:

> A world of searching, the elaboration of a knowledge, on the basis of a systematic experimentation with the bodily functions, a passionate and precise interrogation of her erotogeneity . . . I wished that women would write and proclaim this unique empire so that other women, other unacknowledged sovereigns, might exclaim: I, too, overflow; my desires have invented new desires, my body knows unheard-of songs. (Cixous, 1980, 246)

Neither Cixous nor others with similar views want to suggest that in somatic writing there is any special method or data; rather, they are speaking of an attitude that demands attention to bodiliness "even in purely verbal data."

For an individual signature consistent with this, I suggest a type of union of knower and known. Strange as it may seem, there should be similar intimacy between the governance thinker and what is thought. It is the type of union that administration-think and economics-think and political-behavioralist-think, like much contemporary philosophy-think, does not enjoy. Certainly such a union would strike those concerned with governance techniques as oddly irrelevant, and it is indeed at odds with the desiccated attitude of technicist writing. Some writing on bureaucracy—not all—apes the bureaucracy, for example. More precisely, some writing on bureaucracy apes what-counts-as-bureaucracy. Some writing on economics —not all—apes the way that its field is socially constructed.

Pierre Hadot sheds light on this union of knower and known. He claims that the ancient idea of philosophy as a way of life requires an intimate union of the thinker and what is thought. "In Antiquity, the philosopher regards himself as a philosopher, not because he develops a philosophical discourse, but because he lives philosophically" (Hadot, 1995, 27). The purpose of most ancient philosophy was to transform the philosopher. "The significance and aims of the discourse were conditioned by the ultimate goal of transforming the lives of individuals, of providing them with a philosophical art of living that required nothing less than a . . . metamorphosis" (Hadot, 1995, 23). So he writes of philosophers doing exercises to learn how to live (e.g., bringing oneself back from the worries of living to the simple joy of existing), how to dialogue (e.g., Plato's dialogues and Antisthenes' "ability to converse with myself"), how to die (e.g., contemplation of the whole), and how to read (e.g., ruminate calmly and let the text speak to us). Yes, some modern philosophers like Nietzsche and others may be read in a similar way. Yet it's arguable that in this respect modern philosophy is not as advanced as ancient philosophy.

In seeking such a union, I am speaking of my signature as symbolizing ownership, not merely personal investment, assent, or approval. I am not suggesting nonsense about "finding" my own signature, as if it were a natural form; I am talking about creating. Nor am I suggesting that I should aim for an unchanging signature. More in possession of a signature that unites writer and written, I can write from within my own life's experience and my own body.

Talk of individual signature does reflect dissatisfaction with the limitations of traditional group signatures. Yet the talk does not entail that (a) many individuals and their signatures do not need

WRITING, WITH A DEVIANT SIGNATURE 49

self-improvement, that (b) any person's signature is as good as anyone else's, and that (c) group signatures should be terminated.

There is a downside to talk of individual signature, however. Some thinkers think and act with little sensitivity for the plight of others. Clever people uncleverly can advocate that everyone should pay their bills by Internet or that everyone should read the fine print in purchase agreements, without recognizing that uneducated or senile people cannot easily do that. Rich people can offer suggestions about (say) medical care or retirement planning, without recognizing that poor people have urgent and different wants. Bureaucrats can write bureaucratese, as if everyone were a bureaucrat. This downside is not decisive, however. But it does underscore the desirability (see Essays 7 through 12) of considering the ethical.

A Personal Perspective

Increasingly, I am trying to write from within my body, and I am trying for union of thinker and thought. Yet, my success is limited, mixed on good days. For one thing, I have to struggle against the grain of what I have been taught and what is academically expected—and against my own sense of privacy. On public service, throughout my adult life I have always felt within my body that service to the public is the only activity really worth doing, although once I did a stint in the private sector. I still feel that public service is too limited if it does not set out *to save the world*. I still believe that that is not naive. I have invested my body in much public service employment, and I have introjected strong passions about the value of thinking as playing, justice as seeking, and practice as art.

Clearly, I'm not alone in my discontent for traditional governance group signatures. See the large and vigorous literatures of dissent. For economics, for instance, see the *Biographical Dictionary of Dissenting Economists* (Arestis and Sawyer, 2001); for public administration, see the journal *Administrative Theory & Praxis*. There are many who aspire, under this or that heading, to thinking as playing. People should continue to speak for themselves. Yet I want to say how I have come to believe that thinking as playing is what the doctor ordered. I want to expand an account given before (Farmer, 2003, 419–426) about the relationship of my own thinking to traditional public administration and to economics.

Reflecting on the account, I am impressed by what is left out and by how complicated genuine somatic writing is. I am right to confess my limits. I say nothing about my interest in, and extensive teaching of, history of political theory. There is little even of biographical information. Gibson Burrell (1997) shared with his readers a list of his ancestors back to the Napoleonic Wars. During the Napoleonic Wars, one of my ancestors was dog feeder to the Albrington Hunt. I know he was called Edward, married to Mary; I know also that I would have hated his job. But I know nothing else about him. Maybe Edward went off to the Battle of Waterloo, or maybe he was a draft dodger. Maybe he adhered to a post-Napoleonic theory about how to feed dogs, or maybe he insisted on doing it the traditional way. Not only is it hard to know oneself, but also it is harder to know about influences ingested.

I have gone through three different attitudes, as I pointed out, in the relationship of my thinking to traditional theory. I choose to see them as quasi-evolutionary stages. I called them my white, green, and pink stages, and I asserted that I am now in my pink period.

White Period

In my white period I was a technicist, and I celebrated traditional theories—the administrative-traditional and the economic-traditional. On the administrative-traditional side, I was a systems tinkerer and a general tinkerer. I was genuinely impressed with the capability of systems analysis to ameliorate serious surface-level administrative hurts for short periods. I loved creating and modifying systems. I was also impressed by the power of commonsense rules-of-thumb. When I provided management consulting services for Public Administration Service and the Jacobs Company (Planning Research Corporation) to some forty different governments like the states of Illinois and Pennsylvania and the cities of Los Angeles, Atlanta, Galesburg, Reading, Salt Lake, Durham, Tacoma, and Milwaukee, most of that was systems tinkering. I tinkered in management, organization, personnel, revenue administration, and performance measurement. Coming out of my work for the National Advisory Commission on Civil Disorders (the Kerner Commission), I wrote a technicist booklet about intercity coordination. When I was a division director for the U.S. Department of Justice, much of that was also tinkering. When I was special assistant to the police commissioner in the city of New York (not a cop, I should add), I don't remember anything that was not technicist.

I am still impressed by the fact that every single agency I have ever encountered inflicts surface level hurts by violation of common sense. Too many fire and police agencies still have rotating shifts, for instance; the list is long and obvious. I am impressed by the cleverness of some administrative reports, just as I used to be impressed by my own—so shiny, so watertight—although I do agree that madness has its own watertight logic. I still recognize society's need to worry about short-term balms to heal surface-level hurts. I recognize that getting into the modern age is not a trivial move, and I notice the example Bernard Lewis (2002, 47) offers of the enthusiastic reception given in some quarters of eighteenth-century Islamic society to efficiency in bureaucratic administration. Yes, pale white period commonsense attitudes can ameliorate the human condition. But I came to doubt whether the administrative-traditional rises to the level of the theory that humans need to be humane in the world.

On the economic-traditional side, my original interest—nothing to do with business—was fired by my belief that economic theory can help in changing the world for the better. When I was employed as an economist, the truth is that I never really enjoyed it. Yet I still had faith in the redemptive power of economics. John Maynard Keynes has always been a hero for me, for instance. I never was a believer in neoliberal economics, or economic fundamentalism. For me (see Essay 15), the self-regulating, beneficent, perfect market—the market as a god—lives in the world of the model. It is a prisoner, as it were, of its own constraints. I never could rejoice in what is called the 1980s Washington Consensus, the belief in fiscal austerity, privatization, and market liberalization that Joseph Stiglitz (2002) describes the International Mon-

etary Fund as inflicting on the world. I do not buy what economists sometimes (great rhetoric?) call a minimalist view of
government's role in generating economic well-being.

Yet, even as I celebrated the administrative-traditional surface
tending, I had a secret prejudice that economic theory can help
thinkers and practitioners see longer-term features or constraints
acting on the bureaucratic situation. I never did suppose that
Niskanen or Migué and Bélanger—and the other modelers described in a useful seed catalog like Mueller 2003—saw the "truth"
beneath the surface. Nor was what they saw untrue. What they
achieved was redescribing, describing from another and—for me—
more interesting point of view or framework. Bureaucracy could
now be seen in the context of a glorious theoretical whole. I taught
public choice economics for several years, and I believed that it
offered powerful insights for change—especially where meaning
is the principal concern. I enjoyed creating (1984) what I called a
Conditional Model about the trade-offs of the public and private
interests. This brings up a point. Modeling is very commonsensical;
but lumping it in with traditional administrative theory doesn't
completely work, because models exist—in a way that admin
theory usually doesn't—in a sort of realm of Platonic forms. Model-
building is safe and fun as long as the audience remembers that
the economic theorist lives in the world of the model and that the
so-called real world (ugly name) is touched only where it touches.
Still, I recognized that economics as a tool is valuable (albeit mixed
in value) as a perspective for governance and administration, just
as I think it is hard to understand governance in ignorance of economics. Yet, same comment as before! Economics-inspired insights
do not rise to the level of theory that humanity deserves in our
context. Economic man, as I like to write, is an anemic substitute
for a full-blooded human.

Green Period

In my green period I felt a need for thinking to probe deeper under
the surface about society and governance, and to shift toward a
more philosophical perspective. It seemed odd to me to aim to-

ward mere efficiency, for instance, in a context where we have (in the phrase used by Greg Palast, 2003) the "best democracy money can buy." It seemed odd to me to think of governance in narrow traditional terms, when Palast (for one) finds it necessary to encompass the "governing" foibles of private enterprise as well as public. Yet, in this green period, I saw what I did as subordinate to the spirit of traditional thinking—in the sense that, despite what I said about pragmatism and tinkering, I wrote too much in deference to technicism and use-value. Even when I wrote (1995) about a world (the postmodern world) that lies beyond the traditional modernist world, I was pursuing traditional story lines. One story line harbored the traditional assumption that—for a story about bureaucracy to be told and be publishable—a better alternative that is more useful-for-administrators must be proffered. Maybe a nonlinear or other less familiar pattern was then not a practical option, for the audience or for me. I was motivated by the thought that it was important that traditional thinkers and practitioners have the opportunity to see that their worldview was too limited. My own "mistake" was to cast postmodernism as a useful notion. It is not that the ideas are not useful (of course, they are); the point is that that is not the point. However, I was impressed by traditional unwillingness to snorkel deeper under the surface. Again, I don't see technicist-inspired activity rising to the level of theory that self-actualized humans deserve.

Pink Period

The most important event in my *administrative* life was in 1994 when I started to attend the meetings of the Public Administration Theory Network (www.pat-net.org). The intellectual and emotional support that association members have provided made it possible for me to explore and expand my ideas about governance thinking. "I was hungry, and you gave me bread."

In my present pink period, I do not stand against the aims of my pale white and green periods. I am happy when problems at the surface are handled. But I want to focus on what I am describing in this collection of essays.

The Group Signature

We need to come more in touch with our group signature's *litost* and with the more hopeful sweet spot. Milan Kundera describes and illustrates the apparently untranslatable Czech word. *Litost* is "a state of torment created by the sudden sight of one's own misery" (Kundera, 1996, 167). Kundera illustrates its relationship to power. If a person has *litost* in relation to the less powerful, he will attempt to hurt that person directly. His example is a boyfriend swimming with a girlfriend who is a better swimmer, and the girlfriend forgets herself and swims faster than her boyfriend. His *litost* impels him to strike her, saying that he is afraid for her safety. If a person has *litost* in relation to a person more powerful, he will hurt himself in order to hurt the more powerful person. A student might choose to kill himself or fail his examinations, for instance, in order to hurt his more powerful parents.

Group signature, overlapping with individual signatures, designates the rhetorical style or habits of mind within which a discipline or field thinks or acts. The limits of group signature are virtually indistinguishable from the limits noted in Essay 6, in its description of discourse theory and perspectivalism. My discourse limits constrain, and empower, my thinking and acting.

On the Litost *Side*

The record of underachievement in the disciplines and fields concerned with governance stands in comparison with the splendiferous overachievement of the physical sciences. The contrast is spectacular. Here is understandable ground for *litost*. Yet there are others, like fragmentation.

A caveat should be entered, following Harold Bloom's comment—quoted at the head of this essay—about wisdom and information. There is much information in the governance disciplines and fields. Yet . . .

The fragmented and narrow boundaries of the various governance disciplines and fields limit their effectiveness and hurt society, as suggested in Essays 2 and 6. The fragmentation results in only partial pictures, and this intensifies *litost*. Political science can never give more than a partial picture; nor can economics; nor can any of the other disciplines and fields. Gibson Burrell (1997) points to one example of ineffectiveness when he tells us that organizational studies pay too little attention to the societal production of organizations. This contrasts with the traditional concern, organizational production. Burrell (1997, 25) directs attention to the production of organization rather than to the organization of production.

The existence of limits imposed by group signature is easier to spot in disciplines other than one's own. Would anyone disagree that the rhetoric of modern mainstream economics includes the mathematical, for example, and that this both empowers and also restricts economic thinking? If anyone would disagree about the restricting, probably it would be an economist.

There are other sources of *litost*, like technicism. On technicism, there is sometimes inability to warn and at other times failure to warn. There are forecasting inabilities in economics, for instance. Failure to warn may be more depressing in terms of societal hurt. The hurt was illustrated in 2002 by the systemic accounting scandals at Enron and elsewhere. How much technicist and self-serving effort did traditional professors of accounting spend on preparing new entrants to the accounting profession rather than alerting the public to the larger picture about accounting practices in contemporary business management?

Herbert Simon noticed differences when moving between fields. He described his first field, American Public Administration, as "an academic backwater." Writes Simon (1991, 114), "But my actual research started in an academic backwater: public administration. However important that field was and is to public affairs, it attracted few scholars with real understanding of what research was about, or how to construct the theoretical foundations for an applied field. Viewed by the norms of science, many of the books published in public administration (and management generally) are positively embarrassing. . . ." He later retracted that statement. I think that his retraction was appropriate, and that the standard of "norms of science" is mistaken.

Moving between disciplines like philosophy and economics

presents startling contrasts of signature. I was awarded a Ph.D. in philosophy by the University of Virginia and a Ph.D. in economics by the University of London. Because of this, I have a strong sense of the distinctive habits of mind that are inculcated in professional philosophers and professional economists. Outsiders who write on topics *owned* by these disciplines can appear "amateurish." One reason is that they do not share the rhetorical style of the discipline; they appear odd. In a philosophy department, Socrates can be, as it were, in the next room. No dead economist, no Keynes, is ever so alive in economics.

On the Sweet Spot

Part of the creation of my individual signature should include establishing which part of the institutionalized signature is most liberating for me. Not all parts of an institution are equally good, or equally bad. My view is that institutionalized ways of thinking are most useful either toward their edges or between ways of thinking. Greater creativity can be generated by contemplating ideas of thinkers struggling with assumptions of their tradition—that is, at the edge of their paradigm. Or, even better, the imagination is empowered in the space between disciplines, between points of view.

The birthplace of Western philosophy may be (mis)read as symbolic of the fertility of decentered perspectives. Thales, Anaximander, and Anaximenes of the Ionian or Milesian school philosophized toward an edge of the Greek world, for example. They and others contemplated in what became part of modern Turkey rather than at the mainland center of the Greek world. Vividly I remember wading out into the water up to my neck (dumb move) off a beach on the island of Samos, looking toward what is now Turkey and thinking about the in-between. Then and hurriedly, remembering that there could be sea monsters, I waded back to Samos—home of Pythagoras before he emigrated to the eastern part of the Greek world. Haven't the edges of discourses, like the edges of cultures and group discourses, normally proved abnormally fertile for generating new insights? To move toward the sweet spot within my group signature, I should be open to wading at least toward the edge.

5 • Listen to Symbols

Thinking as playing should be sensitive to symbols and symbolic systems.

> And however important to us is the tiny sliver
> of reality each of us has experienced firsthand,
> the whole overall 'picture' is but a construct of
> our symbolic systems. To meditate on this fact
> until one sees its full implications is much
> like peering over the edge of things into
> an ultimate abyss.
>
> —*Kenneth Burke*

> A rhetorical criticism of economics can perhaps make
> economics more modest, tolerant, and
> self-aware, and improve one of the
> conversations of [*sic*] mankind.
>
> —*Deidre McClosky*

Listen to symbols and symbolic systems; abandon *exclusive* attention to things and systems of things! Thinking as playing should be sensitive to this critical feature of context. Shifting to playing with symbols can transform the thinker and what is thought. These transformations can be expected if Kenneth Burke, quoted above, is right that symbolic systems construct or coconstruct our picture of "reality."

Traditions of Symbolic Analysis

The New Rhetoric and symbolic interactionism suggest the primacy of the symbolic. It is a primacy that governance traditions are uneven in recognizing. Beyond behavioralism in political science, it is more widely recognized; in economics and in administration, marginally.

The New Rhetoric of the twentieth and twenty-first centuries focuses on the symbolic—and on mutuality. More like sociology, it explores how a society gives rise to what is written-and-said and how what is written-and-said helps shape a society. These emphases on the symbolic and on mutuality can be found in the writings of the principal architects of the New Rhetoric, like Kenneth Burke (already mentioned) and Ivor Richards. Burke and Richards are interested in language. Burke writes of the New Rhetoric as "rooted in an essential function of language itself . . . the use of language as a symbolic means of inducing cooperation in beings that by nature respond to symbols" (Burke, 1969, 43). Richards (1936/1965, 5) writes of the New Rhetoric as involving an understanding of the "fundamental laws of the use of language."

Symbolic interactionism, as is well known, also stresses the primacy of symbols. As long ago as 1969, Herbert Blumer explained symbolic interactionism as based on three premises. The first is that humans "act toward things on the basis of the meanings that the things have for them" (Blumer, 1969, 2). The second premise is that "the meaning of such things is derived from, or arises out of, the social interaction that one has with one's fellows. The third premise is that these meanings are handled in, and modified through, an interpretive process used by the person dealing with the things he encounters" (Blumer, 1969, 2). The nature of any thing, any object, consists of the meaning "that it has for the person for whom it is an object" (Blumer, 1969, 11).

Turn now to governance disciplines. In such books as *Politics as Symbolic Action,* Murray Edelman complains that "Americans have been taught to look upon government as a mechanism that is responsive to their wants and upon these in turn as rational reflections of their interests and their moral upbringing and therefore as stable and continuing" (Edelman, 1971, 3). He wants the center of attention to be political symbolizing.

Deborah Stone writes about constructing worlds of political and policy analysis. She opposes the idea that politics is a rational thing or even a thing at all. Stone tells us that a symbol is anything that stands for something else, and a symbol's meaning depends on how people interpret and use it. A symbol can be "an object, a person, a place, a word, a song, an event, even a logo on a T-shirt" (Stone, 2001, 108). As Stone (2001, 108) goes on to say, "Any good symbolic device . . . shapes our perceptions and suspends skepticism, at least temporarily . . . They are means of influence and control." There is a strong connection between symbols and symbolic systems and what counts as common sense.

In a corner of economics there is McClosky discussing the rhetoric of economics. She argues (1998, 23 ff.), for example, that "proofs [*sic*] of the law of demand are mostly literary." (Let's put aside the question of how many proofs constitute proof.) Many practicing economists would be offended by McClosky's claim about the law of demand. As she explains, the claim is an apparent "attack" on belief in the law of demand that is what she calls "the distinguishing mark of an economist" (McClosky, 1998, 25).

The reader may be entertained by McClosky's rhetorical analysis of statistical significance; or she might not. McClosky claims (1998, 112–138) that "statistical significance has ruined empirical work in economics," and that "econometrics confuses statistical and scientific significance." She has a long section that argues that "the rhetorical history of statistics is the source of the difficulty." She fingers R.A. Fisher, who is described as having had a public relations flair, a gift for naming things. She argues that, despite warnings in statistics books, it is hard *not* to confuse statistical significance with the significance of everyday usage, where the latter refers to practical importance.

Traditionally, administration is not widely understood in symbolic terms. For example, American public administration has been described in such terms as language (Farmer, 1995) and storytelling (White, 2000). Jay White reminds his readers of the long history of public policy analysis as involving storytelling, for example, refer-

encing Martin Rein (1976). Also, there have been articles specifically on the symbolic and on rhetoric (Farmer, 2003a; Farmer &
Patterson, 2003). Dvora Yanow (2002 and earlier) has published on
the construction of race and ethnicity in policy analysis. Barbara
Czarniawska (1999, 2004) has written about organization theory in
terms of storytelling and literary genre. Such publications remind
me of isolated swallows flying in what should be summer.

Symbols, Symbols Everywhere

The business executive wears a power suit, a power symbol. She
notes the Dow Jones average, a symbol of today's state of the
economy. Within bureaucracy there is a direct relationship between
height on the organizational ladder and the availability of opportunities for symbolic action. Higher-level officials get more chances
to do all things, including the symbolic. I would like to repeat
some examples I have given. In presiding at an impeachment hearing, the Chief Justice of the Supreme Court designed his own dress,
his own symbol. At the top of his hierarchy, the fire chief in full
uniform is televised at the scene of a fire; a symbolic message is
that he is "in control" and that the fire is as "under control" as it
can be. I remember my police commissioner seeking the symbolic
value of visiting his precincts. He conducted ceremonies to pro-
mote officers and to reward good behavior. He was saluted. The
midlevel director holds "the director's meeting" and all subordinates are expected to attend and be on time—symbols of deference. At the lower end of the ladder, the meter person and the
garbage collector wear symbols in the form of uniforms, with add-
on symbols like flags. Symbolic action occurs at even the hum-
blest level, even if there it takes merely the form of "binging" or
"postal" behaviors symbolically directed against superiors or
against the world in general. Even paint can be symbolic. There is
white on the fire chief's helmet, and there's red—the color of fire,
not water—on the fire (not water) truck. Symbols flourish everywhere in bureaucracy and throughout governance.

A symbol can be read as having a variety of meanings, conscious or unconscious, stable or flickering, obvious or obscure.

Beware the flags behind the boss's desk, a commonplace in the U.S. government! It's not just to express the director's loyalty. Beware the elevated head table at a conference! It's elevated not just to make it easier for the peons to see. Beware the fatherly talk from the agency head, saying that we are all members of a family! It's not just to tell employees that they should act like brothers and sisters. It's also to remind them that he is daddy. Beware the orderly organization chart, showing no uneven nodes of power! It is not just to depict organizational relationships. Beware the beaming director as he stares at her derriere, telling his subordinate what a professional job she has done! Beware the director as he closes the door, telling his workers that he has an "open door" policy! Symbols pile on symbols, often giving mixed and subliminal messages. Things are indeed important, and they *do* require attention. Yet, listen to symbols and symbolic systems!

6 • Truth: Skepticism, Certainly

Skepticism is coherent, as in the form exhibited by the life of Sextus Empiricus. While not committed to skepticism, thinking as playing should be sensitive to limits in knowing. It can distinguish between Big T Truths and what-counts-as-true. What-counts-as-true is limited by language and coshaped by unthoughts. Thinking as playing should anticipate aporia.

> . . . the conviction of certainty is a sure proof of nonsense and extreme uncertainty.
>
> —*Montaigne*

It is sensible to be skeptical about knowing. That is, it is reasonable to be skeptical about certainty in knowing the truth, the whole truth, and nothing but the truth. It is reasonable to be at a loss about Big T Truth, full-throated assertions of absolute and complete Truth. Thinking as playing should recognize what-counts-as-true, what can be called little t truth.

Even here, sadly there are critical limitations. The thinker as player should expect to encounter *aporia*. By *aporia,* I mean that when arguing from a received belief, a conclusion is reached that contradicts either experience or another received belief. This is Aristotle's definition of *aporia,* a word that literally translated means "with no way out." Writing of Sextus Empiricus, Mates (1996, 5) describes *aporia* as "being at a loss, puzzled, stumped, stymied."

Skepticism about justified knowing of Big T Truth cannot be repressed completely by dismissive one-liners like "You know that skepticism is true; therefore skepticism is false." That is easily answered by Empiricus, who did not speak of knowing, as we will see. While not committed to skepticism, thinking as playing shies away from certainties about the absolute truth. Aporia expected!

In the first section of this essay, I discuss and illustrate how discourse or language limits knowing. The second section indicates that what-counts-as-true is socially constructed not only by language but also by features like power, unthoughts, and self-interest. The third section indicates that skepticism about knowing is coherent, illustrating this with the example of Sextus Empiricus.

Truths from a Perspective

The claim bears repeating that each and every human explanation and understanding is from within one perspective or a set of perspectives. We have no nonperspectival, no godlike, vantage point. Or to put it another way, each and every scientific or hermeneutic proposition is made from within a particular discourse or language. This was noted in Essay 4. Following Nietzsche, Heidegger, Wittgenstein, Derrida, and others, we are conscious of perspectivalism, which describes knowing as limited within a complex of perspectives.

What-counts-as-true is the result of a particular vantage point, from within a particular discourse or language. What is understood can be harmful when what-counts-as-true is mistaken for justified knowledge of Big T Truths—the truth, the whole truth, and nothing but the truth, so help me God! It is not denied that Big T Truth exists, and that what-counts-as-true and Big T Truth sometimes can overlap. The issue is whether we can have justified or sure knowledge of the absolute and complete Truth. So, an important distinction here is between absolute and complete Truth and what-counts-as-true.

The character of the discourse or language coshapes what is counted as true. Psychoanalysis privileges much that economics marginalizes; and, as another example, psychoanalysis and economics marginalize much that ethics privileges. By discourse or language (and I am using the two words interchangeably), I mean what Michel Foucault (1972) describes in his account of discourse theory. This theory describes discourses as exhibiting the following seven features. Discourses provide specific ways of viewing our environment; some would want to say that they create contexts. Discourses are interrelated, some sometimes creating subsidiary discourses. Discourses can act in concert, and they shape and rationalize motivations such as self-interest. Discourses are limiting; each filters some information and arbitrarily excludes or marginalizes opportunities for knowing. Discourses are likely to be more beneficial if speakers are aware of the severity of the limitations. Finally, we have limited opportunity to choose our discourse(s).

Compelled to use language, we are condemned to be misunderstood and to misunderstand; so thinks Jacques Lacan. John McTaggart (1866–1925) was a philosopher with an opposite view. He is celebrated for formulating a paradox that he took as disproving the existence of time. I will sketch his paradox, and then indicate that McTaggart's paradox can be seen not as disproving the existence of time but as suggesting the incapacity of language.

McTaggart's paradox begins by describing two features that he thinks time must include—or to put it another way, features that must exist in a world that can include time. The first is that time must contain, or reflect, fundamental ontological differences between past, present, and future *tenses*. This is the tensed (the A-theory) view of time shared by the person-in-the-street and many philosophers, requiring the property of present *simpliciter*. The second is that time must contain, or reflect, no such fundamental ontological differences. This is the tenseless (the B-theory) view of time associated with Albert Einstein and Bertrand Russell, denying a present *simpliciter*. As Einstein wrote, "For us . . . physicists, the distinction between past, present and future is only an illusion, even if a stubborn one." Rather than past, present, and future, the B-theory speaks of earlier and later. For details on how these two features can be fleshed out in terms of three-dimensional and four-dimensional spacetime, see my book (1990) on McTaggart's paradox.

Armed with a few assumptions, McTaggart can then declare a

contradiction. A first assumption is that the law of noncontradiction applies, and so he refuses the dialectical way out that Martin Hiedegger of *On Time and Being* would take (see Farmer, 1990). A second assumption is that if something has a transitory property, it is possible to assert that it has that property, for example, the property of present *simpliciter.* So, McTaggart concludes that there is no such thing as time.

The purported paradox lies not in reality (ontology) but in McTaggart's understanding of language (predication) about that reality. The paradox is in the discourse, the perspective, that misdescribes. I recommended (1990) the predication way out, a move that Robin LePoidevin (1991) described as "Wittgensteinian obscurantism." I argued that an escape is in recognizing the distinction between matters of ontology and of predication, where predication is understood as a logical and not a grammatical topic. (It is a true report of the ontological state of affairs to make the statement, for example, that there is the property of being present *simpliciter.* But, when I predicate of different moments of time the property of being present, I am not predicating something that is the same property. I cannot predicate presentness *simpliciter;* I can predicate the property of being present at t1, if the property is present at t1.) Language liberates in philosophy and governance thinking; also it confines. Such a resolution of McTaggart's paradox can be read as an illustration of the difficulty in language that Jacques Lacan (1977) describes. It can be interpreted as illustrating how language compels the user to misunderstand and be misunderstood.

Some poetic philosophers and philosophical poets—and all of us, including poetic physicists—can play in the hope of yielding language more accommodating of ontology, of what is. The key word is *more!* It is the kind of move that T.S. Eliot attempted about time in his poem *Burnt Norton,* written in awe at the ruins at Fountains Abbey. "Time present and time past, Are perhaps present in time future, And time future contained in time past." Jacques Lacan (see Evans, 1996) tells us that we have to suffer being misheard, misquoted, and misunderstood. Yet, he can go further and tell us that the real is unknowable. For him, the real goes beyond the imaginary and the symbolic. It is unknowable like Immanuel Kant's thing-in-itself. Lacan's *real* is—as he puts it—the impossible to say, the impossible to imagine.

What Counts

What-counts-as-true is shaped not only by language but also by power considerations, by unthoughts, by self-interest, and by other factors like individual and group ignorance. There are difficulties in achieving even little t truths about governance, let alone Big T or nonperspectival truths.

Unreason frequently lives within reason. Consider Kurt Godel and Angus Graham. Godel's Proof is said to have

> proved that it is impossible to establish the internal logical consistency of a very large class of deductive systems—elementary arithmetic, for example—unless one adopts principles of reasoning so complex that the internal consistency is as open to doubt as that of the systems themselves. (Nagel & Newman, 1958, 6)

Angus Graham was a well-known Sinologist who studied Chinese with aims that included understanding Western philosophy better. He selected for a frontispiece Federico Garcia Lorca's words, "The mind has outskirts where the philosopher is devoured by Chinese and caterpillars." Graham (1992, 65) appeals to "the Western chain of oppositions (that), like the Chinese, is at the foundations of thought . . ." He describes differences between reasoning in the West and in Chinese thinking, explaining (for instance) how propositions like "The cat sat on the mat" are not fully intertranslatable. He asserts that the Chinese equivalent, if there were an equivalent, would be false if "the cat sat on a cloth mat" (Graham, 1992, 65).

Then there are thoughts about unthoughts. Add to Godel and Graham such thoughts from Michel Foucault, from the poets of psychoanalysis, and from Karl Marx.

For an account of how power socially constructs what counts as true, recall unthoughts in terms of Foucault's analysis of normalizing and his view that power relations shape what-counts-as-true. Foucault describes the normalizing role of the prison, and he discusses the normalization that proceeds beyond the prison. "Is it surprising that prisons resemble factories, schools, barracks, hospitals, which all resemble prisons" (Foucault, 1977a)? Normalizing can be illustrated by considering what-counts-as-true in such fields as education, social work, psychiatry, and politics. What counts as true, according to Foucault, is what produces the right kind of person and the right kind of behavior. Such truth is not discovered; rather, it is invented in order to produce a normalized person who "fits in." Foucault writes that truth "isn't outside power, or lacking in power: contrary to a myth whose history and functions would repay further study, truth isn't the reward of free spirits, the child of protracted solitude . . . Truth is a thing of this world; it is produced only by virtue of multiple forms of constraint, and it induces regular effects of power" (Foucault, 1980). Foucault's account of power includes the idea, not merely that knowledge is power, but that power is knowledge. What counts as true in a society reflects the society's power relations. There are some, like analytical philosophers, who believe that objective truth can be reached. They hold that "truth distorted by power relations" can be purified, yielding objective truths. Foucault would deny this. For him, power is an inevitable and unavoidable constituent of truth.

Freud, Jung, and Lacan give accounts of how unthoughts socially coconstruct what-counts-as-true. They explain that, typically, our capacity to know is in the grip of unconscious forces over which we do not have complete control. In his first theory of mental structure (the topographical model), Freud divides the mind into three psychical constructs—the conscious, the preconscious, and the unconscious. The unconscious is separated from the conscious by repression, and material from the unconscious cannot enter the conscious and the preconscious without distortion. In Freud's second theory of mental structure (the structural theory), the three agencies of the mind are identified as the id, the ego, and the superego.

Jung and Lacan write of the unconscious in terms of the transpersonal. Jung speaks of the collective unconscious, which consists of all of mankind's shared symbolic and mythological past. Archetypal figures—like hero, mother, the demon—contribute to complexes, the result of archetypes interacting with one's experience. "The collective unconscious seems to be the storehouse of latent memory traces from man's ancestral past, a past that includes not only the racial history of man as a separate species but also his pre-human or animal ancestry as well" (Hall & Lindzey, 1957, 80). Jung's ideas include the stunning claim that the structure of the world we are born into is already inborn within us.

For Lacan, the unconscious is described famously as structured like a language, as the language of the Other. It is transindividual; it is outside. Lacan's is another stunning claim. "The exteriority of the symbolic" is central to the very idea of a person's unconscious (see Evans, 1996).

These two stunning claims remind us that we tend to simplify too much our selves and our epistemological condition. Freud spoke of the "uncanny," but it is hard for reductionists and rationalizers to hear him. As Rosemary Farmer (1997, 72) points out, the "uncanny of the unconscious undermines the comfortable modernist ethos which privileges consciousness, rationality and human autonomy. Psychoanalysis, which speaks of an unconscious over which we have minimal control, is one of the forces which has tended to undermine the Cartesian subject, the autonomous reasoner who controls all of her own actions."

The uncanny character of the unthought is illustrated poignantly by Freud's account of the death instinct. For Freud, by the time of *Beyond the Pleasure Principle* (1961a), the aim of all life is death. He explains that we dance toward the inorganic, no one dying merely by accident. We have only a limited ability to make choices that are uncontaminated by such deep forces. The prospect for escaping into a realm of purely conscious and rational choice appears slight, if not negligible. In such accounts, deep uncontrollable forces shape what for us counts as true.

What counts as true is shaped as well by self-interest, at both the conscious and unconscious levels. Karl Marx suggests the nature and power of the unthoughts that limit and shape what-counts-as-true. He identifies and traces the economic dynamic that he viewed as acting between the society's substructure and the superstructure. Certainly this account has fathered revisions and grandfathered new accounts of the unthought. For example, there are the first-generation members of the Frankfurt school of critical theory, like Max Horkheimer, Herbert Marcuse, and Theodor Adorno. They extended the notion of Marx's revolutionary subject beyond a single group (the proletariat) and broadened the account of the range of oppression well beyond the economic. They offered a paradigm of consciousness, which can be caricatured by saying that one must develop emancipatory or revolutionary consciousness in order to become reconciled with the alienated world. They prepared the way for Jürgen Habermas, leading second-generation thinker, who turns to the central importance of language in shaping what-counts-as-truth.

Skepticism

Skepticism is typically misrepresented. For one thing, it is neither pessimistic nor nihilistic. For another, there are many forms of skepticism. Some positions are limited in their skepticism to certain topics or methods. Some may be skeptical about knowing eternal ethical values. Others may be skeptical about the capacity of human reason to have sure knowledge about, for instance, God or time. Then there are skeptics who are skeptical about all knowledge. For myself, I agree with St. Augustine, who is skeptical about unaided human reason gaining indubitable knowledge about *all* matters of ultimate reality. I mention the deeply religious St. Augustine because some readers may falsely worry that skepticism is antireligious. No, it is neither anti-religious nor pro-religious.

Thinking as playing is conscious of our epistemological limits. While not committed to complete skepticism, such thinkers are wary of loud certainties and they expect to encounter aporia ("with no way out").

I want to explain the odd suggestion that a good model for a skeptic is an ancient philosopher, the imaginative Sextus Empiricus. He suggests that skepticism should be considered a viable option for living. A second-century Greek physician, Empiricus practiced a form of skepticism called pyrrhonism; he authored *The Outlines of Pyrrhonism.* As noted in Essay 4, ancient philosophy was directed not merely at understanding (i.e., not merely at the goal of contemporary academic philosophers) but also at improving the quality of the philosopher's own way of life. For instance, Sextus's pyrrhonism is a way of life *(agoge)* or a disposition *(epoche),* and he believed that his way of life was a good thing that led to peace of mind *(ataraxia).*

A pyrrhonist like Sextus Empiricus withholds assent about whether any proposition *really* is true or false. Encountering whatever phenomena appear, he suspends judgment about what *really* is the case behind or beyond the phenomena, that is, about what is objectively true or false. He even suspends judgment about the truth of his own propositions, like "I suspend judgment" or "Every issue is indeterminate." He has no system of beliefs; he believes nothing to be true or false as descriptions of any world existing independently of his state of mind.

To illustrate what this means and without taking a position on agnosticism, I can imagine an agnostic making a similar claim. An agnostic may recognize that religious talk might help some talkers to survive life's catastrophes, like fear of death and other miseries. "My mother passed away, and is now looking down on me from Heaven." "I know that my Redeemer liveth"—reinforced by Handel's immortal music. The agnostic might consider such talk to be opinion, not knowledge. She might well claim that she finds peace of mind as a surprising consequence of recognizing that she does not *know* such things.

Pyrrhonists find peace of mind, *ataraxia,* in their attitude. Empiricus tells the story of Apelles the painter. Unable to paint the froth on the mouth of the horse in his painting, Apelles gives up and throws his paint brush sponge at the painting. Accidentally, the sponge produces the right effect. Sextus continues:

> So, too, the Skeptics were hoping to achieve ataraxia (peace of mind) by resolving the anomaly of phenomena and noumena, and, being unable to do this, they suspended judgment. But then, by chance as it were, when they were suspending judgment the ataraxia followed, as a shadow follows the body. (Mates, 1996, 93)

The pyrrhonist's behavior is not at all odd. The pyrrhonist willingly assents to propositions that express the present state of his mind. That is, he assents to what appears to him now to be the case. "It appears to me now that X"—where X is whatever now appears to him. For example: "It appears to me now that the gods are good" or "It appears to me now that I am reading about Sextus Empiricus." He gives assent to the present state of his mind. " . . . we say that the criterion of the Skeptic Way is the appearance . . . Nobody, I think, disputes about whether the external object appears this way or that, but rather about whether it *is* such as it appears" (Mates, 1996, 92). On the surface, the pyrrhonist's behavior is similar to anyone else's. When a dog threatens to bite him, for example, the pyrrhonist can climb up a tree or react in any other way that appears to him now to be appropriate. It appears to him now (if it does) that a dog is threatening to bite him and it appears to him now (if it does) that he should climb up a tree. So he can happily climb up the tree, even without any odd speech declarations about "It appears to me now that . . ." He can do so because such a qualification is understood before any of his statements. However, he suspends judgment about whether what appears to him really is completely and wholly *reality as it truly is.*

Benson Mates points to several misconceptions about Sextus Empiricus's pyrrhonism (Mates, 1966, 5–7). Pyrrhonism, he points out, is not a doctrine or set of beliefs. Unlike forms of modern skepticism, it makes no claim that knowledge of an external world is impossible. Yet it is skeptical about all statements, including value judgments.

> [T]he characteristic attitude of the Pyrrhonist is one of aporia, of being at a loss, puzzled, stumped, stymied . . . Unlike doubting, aporia does not imply understanding . . . (T)he Pyrrhonist is at a loss as to whether to classify (claims about the external world) as true, as false, or, more important, as neither. (Mates, 1996, 5)

This is an attitude also recommended for the thinker as player. As in pyrrhonism, the play of post-traditional thinking should embrace "being at a loss, puzzled, stumped, stymied."

II

Justice as Seeking

That nothing of itself will come,
But we must still be seeking?

—*William Wordsworth*

What Is Post-Traditional Justice?

These essays suggest constitutive features of post-traditional justice as seeking wisdom. The seeking is ongoing, and it reaches beyond established parameters.

The first two essays sketch salient features of our contemporary inherited context. The next two describe justice as searching within self and in relation to the other, both for individuals and organizations. The last two essays give examples of seeking justice insights from open-endedness in traditional wisdom and, routinely, from other cultural traditions.

7 • Start with Shakespeare: O Cursed Legacy!

Acknowledge our legacy for justice-seeking. There is aporia. There is a will-to-simplicity. Also part of our legacy, mixed with less influential views, is the centrality in much public ethics of capitalism.

> . . . . O Cursed Spite!
> That I was born to set it right.
>
> —*Shakespeare, Hamlet*

O Cursed Spite! Like Hamlet, we can acknowledge that we inherit a legacy for our justice-seeking. Prince Hamlet's legacy revolved around regicide. His father's ghost had just explained; Hamlet's father, the king, had been poisoned while sleeping in a garden. The murderer was Prince Hamlet's uncle Claudius, who had then married son Hamlet's mother and ascended father Hamlet's throne. Prince Hamlet's legacy, as he interpreted it, was to make sure of the facts of the legacy and then make sure to avenge them. "O Cursed Spite! That [Hamlet] was born to set it right." He acknowledged his legacy, which would litter the stage with corpses and leave the kingdom in the hands of foreigners. Regicide for regicide! He acknowledged, eventually, that he would have to kill the king.

The point is that each generation and each person inherits a legacy of justice situations and constraints that is not chosen and, in Hamlet's case, was not wanted. The legacy is the context for seeking justice, the substance of what needs to be put right and the form of how it can be put right. In practice, substance and form intermingle. Primarily on substance, examples are the issues listed when Jacques Derrida commented on Hamlet's cursed spite complaint (and I gave his entire list in Essay 1). Recall that the issues are complex governance problems, like the growing proliferation of atomic weapons and the bitter economic rivalry between nations. Within public bureaucracy, the hands of cards inherited long ago by the late Luther Gulick and by the later Herbert Simon included handling machinery of government issues like efficiency. The administrative hand inherited nowadays by my reader and me surely includes issues like administratium or the dead hand of bureaucracy. Primarily on form, there are constraints of belief, like political, religious, and moral attitudes that we learned as toddlers. There are also constraints backed by force and consensus. We are born into a system of laws, for instance. The system commands us; it empowers and limits us; it obligates us to obey, under penalty of law.

Justice as seeking is suggested in coping with the substance and form of our legacy. I suggest that justice wisdom lies primarily in the ongoing seeking. I'm not opposed, for instance, to the promulgation of laws and codes that compel obedience in terms of substance and form. But I am opposed to a bureaucratic attitude that supposes that the *end* of the process is legal and ethical prescription, promises of rewards and threats of punishments. Even within a framework of laws, I think that I should accept unlimited personal responsibility to seek justice.

The first section of this essay points to the aporia that is part of our legacy. In the second section, I discuss our inheritance of will-to-simplicity. The third section of the essay claims that central in our justice legacy is capitalism.

Aporia

Justice wisdom must be sought, as it were, in a sea of aporia. Our justice legacy includes complexities and contraries, shaping both substance and form of justice as seeking.

> The mind is fettered; it has no wish to stay where it is,
> because the conclusion does not content it;
> yet it cannot proceed further, because it has
> no means of resolving the argument.

—Aristotle

It will be recalled (from Essay 6) that *aporia* is a Greek word, and it was mentioned that it can be translated as "with no way out." The translation can also be *difficulty, question,* or *problem.* Elegantly enough, Aristotle in his *Metaphysics* described it, in the words at the head of this paragraph, in terms of the mind being fettered. Aristotle did explain that philosophy and mythology begin in wonder that grows out of an aporia or difficulty, and this difficulty is connected with conflicting arguments. I understand that there are different senses of aporia in Aristotle. One connects aporia with the dialectical process, for instance. A sense that I prefer for the purpose of these essays is the "with no way out" image of a state of ignorance where the thinker feels like a prisoner in chains.

Complexities

Complexities abound. Traditional kinds of thinking, to give one example, resist breaking philosophy's virtual monopoly (better, oligopoly) over rational justice talk. Yet, in this e-world of zines, there is a tendency further to decenter the talk. The suggestion is not being made that only philosophers talk about justice. On the contrary, politicians and administrators discuss justice, and newspaper writers and poets speak about ethics. But the discipline of philosophy and the practice of religion make claims to special understandings. It is important to note who is privileged in justice talk. In doing so, recall that the "justice" of one discourse is not quite the same as the "justice" of another discourse.

Part of our legacy is a tendency in the supply of ethical systems to gloss over constraints of time and space and circumstance. Glossing over, not ignoring completely, is the claim here. The Ten Commandment precept "Thou shalt not kill" is a precept that at first sight does not admit circumstances, for instance. It turns out later that the circumstances are important—as when I am in danger of death, when a loved one is in danger of death, when I am in a just war, and so on. To change the example: it may well be that what was reasonable in a philosophy department armchair is no longer reasonable when under intense pressure, for example, when an entire people is threatened with annihilation. I imagine that the story is more complicated. But some may argue that any such flatness in the supply of ethical thinking can be blamed on theo-philosophical origins, where a divine being (like Zeus) and a divine abode (like Heaven) are considered to be above time and space and constraining circumstances.

Our legacy of contemporary justice talk seems awkward in embracing a world where, in Novalis's phrases, "light and darkness mate" and "geometric diagrams and digits are no longer the keys to living things" (Novalis, 2000). It seems gauche in a world where light and darkness metastasize as if out of control—where astronauts venture into space triumphs, seniles rot in nursing homes, new Internet capabilities flood the market, planners plan defense with space weapons of mass destruction, new medical procedures lengthen lives, and fat children munch in fast-food stores. It seems foreign in speaking with diagrams and digits about situations where good and bad merge, forgetting that it is only psychological splitting that pronounces people as either heroes or nothings. Our legacy of contemporary justice talk is awkward in embracing a world that is hotfooting faster and faster—a world of power and paralysis, of finitude and aporia. As an analogy for our eth-talk legacy, it is as if we had an astrophysical theory that was excellent for "Euclidean space" but that did not hold for the curvature of space-time.

Contraries

Contraries abound in our justice legacy. Central is the matter of objectivity and subjectivity, for example. On the one hand, those with loved ones killed in the World Trade Center on September 11 may think that it is inconsistent with leading a fully human life to give up the possibility that their justice claims are objective and independent features of the world, as opposed to being nothing more than subjective reactions like emotional outbursts. They may well reject the idea that their ethical judgments of disapproval are no more than subjective opinions. Their intestines would find it difficult to live with the weak beer of subjectivity. I agree with them. Subjective ethics are weak beer. On the other hand, however, it is not at all clear how we can decisively identify firm and compelling grounds for objective moral claims. Essay 8 explains that no single justice system has a decisive claim over others as *the* right system. No decisive understandings are available about the grounds on which moral judgments can be justified. Claiming otherwise is even weaker beer.

Many are the other contraries. For a sample, notice this "knot" from psychiatrist R.D. Laing:

> A son should respect his father,
> He should not have to be taught how to respect his father.
> It is something that is natural.
> That's how I have brought up my son anyway. (1970)

Will-to-Simplicity

Yet, falsely, our legacy is that simple justice should be simply obvious; justice talk should be uncomplicated. This too shapes substance and form.

This will-to-simplicity is reflected in an oversupply of strident moral systems, self-described as common sense, for example, political, religious, and other nostrums. God said . . . , history teaches . . . , our political system, the best in the World, maintains . . . , we in this society believe . . . , we the greatest generation hold . . . and so on.

Will-to-simplicity is encouraged by the aggressive decisiveness of some ethics advocates, well-meant posturing. Consider the distinguished philosopher R.M. Hare, for example. Pontificates Hare (1989, 4), "Although I have been hard on philosophers of other persuasions than my own, I would not dream of excluding them from the schools, provided that they were prepared to exercise a similar restraint." Hare dismisses John Rawls and Robert Nozick, no less philosophers than he. "The truth is that if one puts philosophers of this sort in some role in the legislative process, they will only do what my first class of analytical philosophers would do, namely dress up as philosophy the political convictions which they had prior to any of their philosophical reasoning" (Hare, 1989, 3–4). Not only philosophers jump, decisively, to supply.

Administrative ethics gallops in. "Forget ethics" has been a popular, implicit brand line. This was the line implicit in the fact-value dichotomy swallowed raw by Herbert Simon, as mentioned before. Long after this dichotomy had fallen out of favor in philosophy, Simon's reliance on logical positivism for his foundational *ethical* insight remained current in traditional administrative thinking. Instrumentalism has been a second brand line. It focuses on the ethics of the ways that bureaucrats work in order to achieve the objectives that are set for them rather than on the justice of the objectives themselves. Because the instrumental is primary to practice as practice-is-now-socially-constructed, the confinement of the ethical to the instrumental is seductive. However, it is a seductive limitation.

Cultural foundation has been a third brand line, and Essay 8 discusses why it is phony. Such foundations can be in the form of comforting sayings that function like proverbs, for example, she is a good soldier, or she has done what she was trained to do. Or, they can be comforting rationalizations. Some are trivial, like the rationalization that oath-taking explains the creation of moral obligation, that is, that taking an oath (see Lewis, 1991) provides an ample grip or foundation for moral, not just legal, obligation to execute the law.

The idea that justice claims should be simple is also encouraged on the demand side. Economics, but not ethics, can be a difficult subject. Physics, but not metaphysics, can be complicated. Martin Heidegger complains about this misunderstanding. He notes that few in his audience would complain if they experienced Werner Heisenberg speaking on theoretical physics as not immediately intelligible. "Not so with the thinking that is called philosophy" (Heidegger, 1969/1972, 1). A variety of cultural prejudices and attitudes contributes to the expectation that justice or ethical inquiry should be an archaeology of the obvious, a project of making common sense conscious. For instance, there's the view—as old as Aristotle and other ancient Greeks—that whatever is believed by all about ethical behavior is ethical.

Capitalism

The dynamic component at the center of contemporary public justice thinking in the advanced industrial countries is belief in capitalism. In the United States, capitalism is often called the American Way. It is at the heart of our legacy, shaping the substance and form of orthodox day-to-day thinking. This component then fuses with other belief systems. Sometimes it is more or less dominant, but rarely is it absent.

Capitalism as a moral text tends to fall between disciplinary cracks. For moral philosophy, capitalism is the province of another discipline. For economics, moral philosophizing is also in the province of another discipline.

Yet the case can be made that capitalism—or consumerism or the free market, to give it more appealing names—is a principal component of civic religion. It brings to the mix faith and ethical commitment, and a vast population of believers. It possesses the equivalent of cathedrals in corporate office buildings and of churches in malls. CEOs are given adulation that saints would envy. Free market economics is a kind of theology. The comparisons could go on.

The case should not be oversimplified, neither in relation to justice-think nor religion-think. Contemporary justice-think, for example, is hodgepodge, as values come to the fore and recede in response to happenings—including reaction to hyperreality like that displayed in the media. Certain relatively fixed attitudes are conscious, like belief in a particular political party or religion. Some are primarily unconscious, like a tendency to scapegoat. Or they can be both conscious and unconscious, like nationalism and capitalism. People wave flags and make other group gestures, and speak loudly of their love of country. Jingoism grasps people as if they were puppets, for instance; the pack animal tendencies of people kick in, and it is us versus them.

Christianity, Judaism, and Islam, and other religions propound ethical systems that have a profound impact. They usually speak against Mammon and what is worldly, but they tend to be intertwined with the market. Weber speaks of the Puritan belief that a sign of the identity of those predestined for Eternal Bliss is commercial success on earth, a conflation as preposterous as the selling of indulgences. Yet, the power of capitalism should not be denied. Capitalism moves not only mountains but also entire corporations. The Ten Commandments have a reverence, even in the breach; but the Dow Jones average also has its devotees.

Then there are other justice and justice-related components, powerful but with a narrower following. Examples are belief in animal rights and belief in the ecological, powerfully motivating for followers but at this time not on the same scale as the large religions. Then there are the channeling ideologies, like the political. In the United States, the framework of Republican and Democrat is significant in shaping norms, where taboo are thoughts that can be labeled socialist or liberal. In Great Britain a parallel framework is Labor, Conservative, and Liberal. Supporting and infusing these political ideologies are ethical "theologies." Varieties of libertarian ideologies can be underlain by Robert Nozick's account of justice, for example; varieties of liberalism can involve accounts like John Rawls's.

Other legacy components are network(s) of historical events, both group and individual. The ethical legacy is shifted when a group experiences economic weakness or when another group is militarily dominant. It changes for an individual, for instance, when hormones are firing or when there is an addiction.

Yet such events and everyday back-and-forth moral chat is permeated by capitalism. But important is what counts-as-capitalism, not what capitalism actually is. For example, some will believe in the presence and efficacy of the free market, even where it is absent. Think about international trade, where it has been said that one-third of the trade is not free but between branches of the same multinational corporations (e.g., see Martin & Schumann, 1998, 112).

To the extent that our legacy of justice ethics incorporates capitalism, there is powerful endorsement for pursuing self-interest. Capitalism did not invent self-interest. Merely, its embrace breathed hyperlife into selfishness, properly understood. To the extent that it is central in public ethics in advanced industrial societies, our legacy lessens hope in such values as altruism, love, and public interest motivation. O Cursed Spite!

8 • Justice Systems:
More in Heaven and Earth?

Avoid canned solutions. Justice systems are indecisive, for example, if one seeks conclusive, rational evidence that any one system is *the* right system. Indecisiveness is also reflected in meta-ethics and in the so-called hermeneutic turn. This is also our legacy.

> The value of philosophy is, in fact, to be sought largely in its very uncertainty. The [person] who has no tincture of philosophy goes through life imprisoned in the prejudices derived from common sense, . . . To such a man the world tends to become definite, finite, obvious; common objects rouse no questions, and unfamiliar possibilities are contemptuously rejected.
>
> —*Bertrand Russell*

> There are more things in heaven and earth, Horatio, Than are dreamt of in your philosophy.
>
> —*Shakespeare, Hamlet*

Like cigarette packages, perhaps justice systems should carry warning labels. *Warning: Beware of off-the-shelf systems!* Justice has a vast literature within moral philosophy, and a striking feature of this literature as a whole is its indecisive outcome. The long history of justice thinking is replete with excellent arguments that have been advanced for contrary and contradictory justice systems. No system for making justice decisions, as hinted in Essay 7, has a decisive claim over others as *the* single, right system.

Hamlet might have been suggesting (see quote above) that what is in heaven and earth exceeds not just Horatio's system but any philosophical system. Packing justice impulses and ideas into philosophical systems distorts even as it liberates, inexorably. By *justice system,* I mean a complete set of decision criteria for what is just—or ethical, moral, right, or good. Deontological systems, for instance, speak of ethics as duty. Consequentialist systems, like the utilitarian, appeal to the greatest enduring benefit for most people. Intuitional systems differ in relying on what is intuitively understood. Ethical egoist systems differ again in describing as ethical what promotes best the greatest enduring benefit for me. Cultural relativist systems turn to what is usually done in a society, and subjectivist systems hold that the ethical is what I prefer or like. A religious system—like the Christian, Jewish, and Islamic—typically maintains that what is ethical is what is divinely commanded. As implied, there are varieties within systems.

Justice wisdom accrues primarily from the ongoing searching. I suggest that there is a need for justice-seeking to reach beyond systems to the poetic. Uncertainty is part of knowing justice, perhaps oddly. Listen to Bertrand Russell quoted above, a philosopher who explains the practical relevance of uncertainty and, by implication, of searching. Yet this is hard for those with attitudes that need the antidote of what Russell calls "a tincture of philosophy."

Recognizing Indecisiveness in Justice Systems

Considered as a whole, the entire corpus of justice claims exhibits a marked style. Indecisiveness of outcome is the striking stylistic feature. This megastyle of the entire product differs from the varying styles of particular thinkers or groups of thinkers. The product here is the whole body of justice thinking stretching over several millennia, from Homer, Mencius, and Genesis to the present day. The long history of justice thinking—whether philosophical, political, or religious—is replete with conflicting claims. Excellent arguments have been, and can be, advanced for excellent contrary and contradictory views.

It is an undecidedness that contrasts with the decisive assertiveness, even aggression, of many particular justice claims. Here is Homer. "The hero [Agamemnon] spoke like this, and bent the heart of his brother [Menelaos] since he urged justice. Menelaos shoved with his hand Adrestos the warrior back from him, and powerful Agamemnon stabbed him in the side" (Homer, *The Iliad*). Justice ("dike") is understood as vengeance and retribution, as Agamemnon "came on the run" to join his brother and speak "his word of argument." Here is Genesis. "Because the cry of Sodom and Gomorrah is great, and because their sin is very grievous, I will go down now, and see whether they have done altogether according to the cry of it, which is come unto me; and if not, I will know" (Genesis, 18:20–21). Justice is understood as divine retribution.

Views diverge about both the material and the formal nature of justice. I have just mentioned justice as retribution and revenge. Other views include justice as social harmony, as mercy, as desert, as impartiality, as mutual advantage, as reciprocity, as fittingness, as fair distribution and exchange.

Rawls, Nozick, and Smart

Rawls's, Nozick's, and Smart's views on justice, taken as a whole, provide an illustrative sample of the undecidedness of the entire corpus of justice claims.

John Rawls advances a liberal theory of justice (Rawls, 1971), although he later—as indicated below—took a hermeneutic turn. He gives an end-state account of justice as fairness. Rawls's theory certainly is important, triggering a renaissance in political philosophy (Buchanan, 1980, 5). Rawls starts from a mind game that involves rational individuals making decisions behind (in his celebrated phrase) a "veil of ignorance"—not knowing any personal details like their own conceptions of the good, their special psychological propensities, and their status in terms of their sex, wealth, race, and age. He goes on to develop two principles that should govern the basic structure of society and that he believes that people in such an original position would agree upon. The first is that "each person is to have an equal right to the most extensive system of equal basic liberties compatible with a similar system of liberty for all" (Rawls, 1971, 250). The second is that "social and economic inequalities are to be arranged so that they are both (a) to the greatest benefit of the least advantaged, and (b) attached to offices and positions open to all under conditions of fair equality of opportunity" (Rawls, 1971, 302–303). From this analysis, he thinks that he is able to draw conclusions such as that injustice "is simply inequalities that are not to the benefit of all."

Robert Nozick proposes a libertarian theory of justice, a very different prescription from Rawls's. He maintains that the "complete principle of distributive justice would say simply that a distribution is just if everyone is entitled to the holdings they possess under the distribution" (Nozick, 1974, 64). This view he considers captured in his three principles about justice in holdings. The first principle is that a "person who acquires a holding in accordance with the principle of justice in acquisition is entitled to that holding." He develops this understanding by embracing Locke's view that original ownership of an unowned object originates in mixing labor with the object. The second is that "a person who acquires a holding in accordance with the principle of justice in transfer, from someone else entitled to the holding, is entitled to the holding." His third principle is that "no one is entitled to a holding except by [repeated] applications" of the first two principles. From his analysis, Nozick (1974) thinks that he is able to reach conclusions such as the "minimal state is the most extensive state that can be justified" and that any "state more extensive violates people's rights."

J.J. Smart evaluates justice claims on a utilitarian basis (Smart & Williams, 1973), offering a prescription different from both Rawls's and Nozick's. A utilitarian, Smart does not understand justice to be a fundamental moral concept. The "concept of justice as a fundamental ethical concept is really quite foreign to utilitarianism. A utilitarian would compromise his utilitarianism if he allowed principles of justice which might conflict with the maximization of happiness (or more generally of goodness) . . ." (Smart, 1991, 106). However, Smart does express interest in justice "in a subordinate way, as a means to the utilitarian end" (Smart, 1991, 107). For him, what matters is "that the total amount of happiness is maximized."

Meta-Ethics as Indecisive

Diverging views also concern whether and how justice is an objective feature of what is, whether and how it requires grounding
in the divine, whether and how it can be grounded in reason,
whether and how it can be satisfactorily grounded in a language or
a culture or a way of life, whether it needs any grounding, whether
talk about justice could be better served by focusing on injustice,
and so on. The divergence extends much further.

Recall the description in the introduction about the formal nature of justice. "Justice" as a concept can be understood in the
traditional sense to refer to the minimum that each person should
consider that she owes to other people, not as a matter of law, love,
politeness, or prudence but of what morally ought to be the case.
This characterization is a good starting point in thinking about
justice. It should be seen as open to modification, however.

Some do indeed object to the very idea of justice, holding (like
the utilitarians) that there are better conceptualizations. Some feminist positions (certainly not all) regard justice talk as inappropriate. Carol Gilligan, for instance, distinguishes an ethic of care from
an ethic of justice, and she holds that they are "fundamentally in-
compatible" (Gilligan, 1982). "The conception of morality as concerned with the activity of care centers moral development around
the understanding of responsibility and relationships, just as the
conception of morality as fairness ties moral development to the
understanding of rights and rules" (Gilligan, 1982, 19). For her,
justice is a male-dominated voice.

Some Marxists also object to the very idea of justice, although
a second strand of Marxism accepts liberalism's emphasis on justice but not its belief that justice and private ownership of the means
of production are compatible. Some Marxists believe that justice
is not something the good community needs; they disagree with
Rawls that justice is the first virtue of social institutions. As
Kymlicka explains, they see justice as appropriate only if we are
in the "circumstances of justice" where there are conflicting goals
and limited resources. For them, justice "is a regrettable necessity
at present, but a barrier to a higher form of community under con-

ditions of abundance. It is better if people act spontaneously out of
love for each other, rather than viewing themselves and others as
bearers of just entitlements" (Kymlicka, 1990, 166).

Philosophy in General: Progression?

Let me recap. Each ethical system has its strengths and weaknesses.
Each is attended by supporting arguments, counterarguments,
counter-counterarguments. Some may advocate, say, deontology as
the basis for moral choices; others may assert the claims of, say,
consequentialism; others may argue for or against, say, "balancing
up" both alternatives. Each option has well-known difficulties, and
honest disagreement "ought" to be respected. There is no outright
winner. In this way, a feature of our understanding of justice can be
described as indecisive in outcome.

It may be objected that this feature should not be called striking, however, because it is one common throughout philosophy.
The feature is common no less, beyond moral philosophy, in epistemology and metaphysics. It is common not only in the sense that
it is general but also in that it could hardly be otherwise to the
extent that it is right and meaningful to conceptualize philosophy
as an "untamed science"—a study that, by its nature, cannot have
rules for deciding that are beyond questioning.

That justice claims as a whole should have the megastylistic
characteristic of being undecided is no surprise if Bertrand Russell
and others can agree (as they should) that there has been a lack
of knowledge progression in the history of philosophy. Even
though there is nothing in current and previous discussions of
justice or philosophy to suggest that progression will occur in
the future, lack of progressivity should not be taken to imply that
there is no value in philosophical discussions of justice. Certainly, there is value.

Indecisiveness in Culture-Based Systems

Further suggestive of this undecidability is what Georgia Warnke
calls the hermeneutic turn in thinking about justice in political

philosophy (Warnke, 1993). This turn has been moving away, in recent years, from seeking universalistic solutions toward searching for answers within particular cultures or ways of life.

Rawls is an example of a celebrated thinker who took a hermeneutic turn. In 1971 he argued for his conclusions grounded on a universalistic appeal to neutral procedures of rational choice; later he shifted to base his justice principles on a Western or Anglo-American way of understanding freedom and equality. Warnke explains that "many important political theorists no longer try to justify principles of justice or norms of action on what might be called Kantian grounds" (Warnke, 1993, vii). That is, they no longer appeal to universalistic grounds like formal reason, the character of human action, or the neutral procedures of rational choice. Rather, "these philosophers suggest that if a society wants to justify its social and political principles it can do so simply by showing their suitability for it, that is, by showing that these principles express the meanings of the society's goods and practices, history and traditions" (Warnke, 1993, vii). She explains that John Rawls argues for the "faithfulness and congruence" of his account of justice to settled convictions of his society (Rawls, 1993, 518); Michael Walzer appeals to social understandings of his society (Walzer, 1983, 8); and Charles Taylor bases his views on the intersubjective meanings of his society (Taylor, 1985).

This reliance on core values has long been an interest in action fields like public administration. There has been the rationalization that public administrators are obligated to support "core values" or "the enduring values of public administration" (e.g., see Denhardt, 1991). The system of core values has special emotional, if not reflective, appeal for public administration thinking. For one thing, it gives permission to keep on doing whatever was being done.

We should underscore why a hermeneutic turn in political philosophy reinforces the present claim that a stylistic feature of the entire corpus of justice thinking is its undecidability. Much discussed in the philosophy of science is the idea that any faithfulness and congruence of an interpretation or theory with a set of observed facts cannot rule out important alternative interpretations or theories. Recall the Duhem-Quine thesis, noted in Essay 1, on the underdetermination of theories. The thesis includes the claim that there is always an indefinite number of theories capable of accounting for any set of observed facts. Regardless of the volume of contrary evidence, any of these theories can be sustained if radical enough adjustments are made in auxiliary hypotheses. If the Duhem-Quine thesis is correct, there are an indefinite number of theories of justice that can account for the set of facts in the selected culture or way of life.

Turn now to the problem of reconciling interpretations, an issue much discussed. Recall Warnke's argument that there "is no one 'correct' or exhaustive view of a given society's meanings; nor is there a set of standards or procedures that could guarantee our agreement on one canonical interpretation of them" (Warnke, 1993, 11). Her argument is that just "as we can have different understandings of a literary text, in a democratic society we can have different plausible and even workable interpretations of our own political traditions and social life" (Warnke, 1993, 11). Recall the differing views of Karl Apel and Hans Gadamer on the status of interpretations (e.g., Apel, 1981; Gadamer, 1989). Apel holds the optimistic view that each successive interpretation is a better understanding. Gadamer has a pessimistic view that each successive interpretation is a different understanding.

The rationalization about cultural core values has, as noted, weak cognitive appeal as a system for grounding bureaucratic action. Even less appealing on reflective grounds is the view that such core values can be known without ongoing searching. During any war, some will hold that a core patriotic value is not to question governmental policy; others will hold that a core patriotic value is the right to question. Seems to require searching! So pumped up are we about belonging to our nation or to our group that it is natural to think that *the* system of values (as if there were only one) expressed in the history of our group is of prime significance. It is easy to overlook the changes in our culture over time and the differences between the subcultures within our culture. It is easy to overlook the claim that the dichotomy between core and peripheral values can be deconstructed. We can forget that a core value of the United States at one point was to maintain slavery, for example, some saw slavery as a biblical obligation. Nowadays most would agree that it's unethical to suppose that anyone could be obligated—as a moral, and not just legal, obligation—to support slavery. It was once a core value that a wife should be subordinate to her husband. Nostalgia for the good old days, or for the days of our youth, is a weak foundation.

A Note on Religion

The inclusion of religious systems will pain some readers, especially in countries like the United States and Saudi Arabia. The religious situation is complicated by the existence of unbelievers and by the strength of some conflicting views held by different religions. But all I am suggesting is that religious systems, no less than philosophical systems, are supported by excellent arguments and opposed by excellent counterarguments.

Some are willing to subject their religious beliefs to rational analysis; many others are not. Deanna Laney is reported (Springer, 2004) to have believed that God wanted her to kill her three children who ranged in age from eight years to fourteen months. As she murdered them, she found it increasingly difficult. She is quoted as saying that "I thought it was the Lord saying to me, 'You're just going to have to step out in faith. This is faith. You can't see why. You just got to.'" In taking a step not unlike the test that Abraham "passed" when God is reported to have asked him to sacrifice his son, Laney might be considered irrelevant because in April 2004 she was acquitted by reason of mental illness. Many religious believers are entirely rational, and some are great thinkers (e.g., St. Augustine). However, Laney's story does underscore what we knew already from Freud (1975), that often religious views are based on nonrational considerations. But the thrust of this essay is to speak of religion insofar as it is a matter not of faith but of rational analysis.

Reverend Barry Lyn, director of Americans United for the Separation of Church and State (www.au.org, September 21, 2003) reports that there are 20 million unbelievers in the United States, and the same Barry Lyn reports that there are in the United States, for instance, two thousand different religions. Regardless of such differences, believers usually hold that religion meets the criteria to be declared a clear winner in any contest of ethical systems. They would affirm or assume—to revert to Philosophy 101 material—three propositions necessary for such a victory. These are that God does exist, that God is a credible moral authority, and that we have (or someone has) reliable access to God's opinions on ethical matters. But, of course, others would not, and they would disagree vehemently. Among philosophers, David Hume is but one who would reject such claims, and I don't know how his arguments could be simply dismissed. As a purely rational matter, there seem to be excellent arguments for the religious position and equally excellent counterarguments.

Epilogue

Searching for simple justice is not simple. Justice as seeking should include sympathetic reflection on the content of the justice systems that are within the literature of moral philosophy. It also should include reflection on ideas available in other traditions, for example, religious, political, and psychological, and on insights available in arts like poetry and novels. But Bertrand Russell's advice here is critical. He explains why philosophy should be studied—not for the sake of definite answers, but rather for the sake of the questions themselves; no definite answers, he notes, as a rule can be known to be true. He continues that

> these questions enlarge our conception of what is possible, enrich our intellectual imagination and diminish the dogmatic assurance which closes the mind against speculation; but above all because, through the greatness of the universe which philosophy contemplates, the mind also is rendered great, and becomes capable of that union with the universe which constitutes its highest good. (Russell, 1959, 5)

Justice as seeking does not look for ready and definitive answers from canned systems.

9 • Self, with Style

Searching within my self is a critical part of justice thinking, both for humans and for human organizations. Yet it is difficult partly because what is within is socially constructed. Create my own style, which Nietzsche describes as shaping values. Recognize that this is a reciprocal movement between the self and the other.

My life is my message.

—*Mahatma Gandhi*

Two things fill my mind with ever new and increasing admiration and awe, the oftener and more steadily we reflect on them: the starry heavens above and the moral law within.

—*Immanuel Kant*

"The starry heavens above and the moral law within . . ." With this lilting and poetic phrase, Immanuel Kant (1997, 133) summarizes his impression that the moral-law-within can be known with assurance. It's straightforward! Not even veiled in darkness! As he writes, "I have not to search for them (the starry heavens above and the moral law within) and conjecture them as though they were veiled in darkness or were in the transcendent region beyond my horizon; I see them before me and connect them directly with the consciousness of my existence." Of the moral law, he announces that it "begins from my invisible self, my personality, and exhibits me in a world that has true infinity . . ." He proclaims that this assured seeing of the moral-law-within "infinitely elevates [his] worth as an intelligence" and reveals to him "a life independent of animality and even of the whole sensible world . . ." (Kant, 1997, 133). Unfortunately, I don't think that picking out a "moral-law-within" is straightforward. It is a huge problem!

Yet I want to suggest that searching within the self is a critical part of justice-seeking for individuals and even for bureaucracies. Embrace the aporia! For the reasons given in Essay 3, a start should be made with the language of the self. For a public or private bureaucracy, a start can be made with the language of bureaucracy.

Friedrich Nietzsche and others, it seems to me, can help in choice of style both for my self and for bureaucracies. So can searching that contemplates a reciprocal movement between self and other. It's a movement between a justice-seeker and her other; it's between a bureaucracy and nonbureaucracy, between a corporation and noncorporation.

This essay focuses on the first part of this reciprocal movement. The first section of this essay discusses searching-within, and the second speaks of style. "To thine own self be true" is the advice in *Hamlet* of Shakespeare's Polonius to his son. Outside should match what is inside the son. At his most sublime, the composer Mozart projects outward from the inside of his very being. Inside is outside in his music. As in art, so in justice-seeking!

Searching-Within

Searching-within can be understood as searching for the singular energy that some call spirituality. Others use terms like self-realization; I have called it poetry. Much bunk is spoken about spirituality, and spirituality is often mistaken as an easy way for the shallow to be deep. We can only try to avoid such pitfalls.

The purpose of the searching is to identify what should motivate my whole being. It is not limited, for example, to finding out how I feel/think. Cardinal John Henry Newman's distinction between notional and real assent helps make the point. Notional assent is affirming an understanding in a purely abstract way, such as the assent I might give to my regret on hearing a television story about a fatal accident on I-95 or the schoolboy-like assent I give to the economic law of diminishing marginal utility. For Newman, real assent engages my entire being. My assent engulfs and permeates my head, my heart, my guts. I compare my assent to the truth about the death on I-95 with my assent to the truth about the death of my father Joseph. I acknowledge the death of my father with an intensity that still fills my being. Although less intense as the years have passed, his death is still more than vivid. For more on the distinction, see Newman's *Grammar of Assent* (1979).

Spirituality can be specified in terms of *immaterial assets*. Robert Fogel, winner of the 1993 Nobel Prize in economics, does so. He argues that the most intractable maldistribution in the rich countries is in spiritual, not material, assets. As he writes, it is necessary

> to address such postmodern concerns as the struggle for self-realization, the desire to find a deeper meaning in life than the endless accumulation of consumer durables and the pursuit of pleasure, access to the miracles of modern medicine, education not only for careers but also for spiritual values, methods of financing an early, fruitful, and long-lasting retirement, and . . . (Fogel, 2000, 176–177)

Clearly, some people are more deficient than others.

Fogel speaks of spirituality in terms of self-realization (his first item). Self-realization is what spirituality leads toward, according to Fogel; it is not merely fulfilling one's desires. To Fogel as to Aristotle, the self-realization of spirituality includes "the fullest development of the virtuous aspects of one's own nature" (Fogel, 2000, 206). Also, self-realization is "a particularized creative project of individual growth" (Fogel, 2000, 205). Self-realization should be understood in terms of fifteen spiritual resources, according to Fogel. They are a sense of purpose, a vision of opportunity, a sense of mainstream work and life, a strong family ethic, a sense of community, a capacity to engage with diverse groups, an ethic of benevolence, a work ethic, a sense of discipline, the capacity for focusing and concentrating one's efforts, the capacity to resist the lure of hedonism, the capacity for self-education, the thirst for knowledge, an appreciation for quality, and self-esteem. Fogel's list is a useful indication of the general nature of spirituality.

Yet, the list may be questioned. For one thing, it is arbitrary to say that a strong family ethic is an "essential" part of spirituality. Certainly families are nice, just as the comforts of gangs, fraternities, and countries are nice. But to claim that a strong family ethic is essential seems over the top; I imagine that Fogel must be implying that God or a saintly hermit could not be very spiritual unless he or she has a family. For another thing (see Essay 17), it is arbitrary to exclude love.

For myself, I have explained spirituality as referring to the presystematized energy within an individual person. It is somewhat like an "id" before the id was named and classified as the property of psychology. This spiritual energy can be described as poetic or sublime; as revolutionary; as ineffable; as exceeding bounds; and as an opening of the person to the wholeness of herself—and then as an opening to the other, for example, to the wholeness of nature and sociality. Calling it "spirituality" has the severe disadvantage of implying what is thought of as the sacred. I don't exclude what is religious or sacred; but I am not referring to, or limiting it to, religion. I still prefer the term "poetic." But that too has disadvantages, one being that it does not convey to many the idea of gripping a person within her entrails, within the cockles of her heart.

Spirituality in persons is the energy included in a broad understanding of self-actualization. Self-actualization is being all that you can be as a human. For self-actualization, I take it that humans flourish in directions that include the biological, psychological, social, spiritual, ethical, and other dimensions. Notice that I have broadened this list of dimensions to include the ethical; I don't want to limit the range of dimensions. Also, interactions between the dimensions are transactional rather than interactional or reductionist (see R. Farmer, 1999). That is, it's neither a matter of considering each dimension in isolation (reductionist), nor thinking in terms of one dimension acting on one or more of the others (interactional). In a transactional view, the character of each dimension is constituted in simultaneous interaction with all the others. Libido, for instance, is implicated in each and all of the dimensions. The embodied human being is not a mere biological entity, any more than she is a mere spiritual or mere psychological entity. Nor is it an interacting set of such features.

Spirituality, also, is not something opposed to the body. Some call it embodied or corporeal spirituality precisely because they stand opposed to the notion of the spiritual as apart from, or opposed to, a person's body (as in, say, St. Augustine). It is embodied in the general sense intended by Maurice Merleau-Ponty (1962, 146). In a phrase I admire, he writes that "The body is our general medium for having a world." The body is our general medium for having the world of justice-seeking. The form of embodiment depends on processes of social construction, it can be added.

My description of spirituality refers to an individual, but not to a solitary person. As the social dimension is intended to indicate, the description refers to a person in communion with others. Also, it does not refer to a person separate from her environment. I should repeat the point made in Essay 3 that there is a necessary relationship between a person and her environment, for example, in the sense that the air of the environment can be described as "part" of the functioning lungs.

Spirituality, for me, involves a seeking to be more spiritual than I am—more poetic than the little I am. It is more than simple fulfillment. The self-actualization includes overcoming myself. This view has features in common with Nietzsche's *Ubermensch* (overman, superman) and with some religious ideas about personal rebirth. But I don't want to make those comparisons. Both comparisons have too much baggage. The term "superman" is often misunderstood as being the opposite of what Nietzsche intended, for example.

Public and private bureaucracies, no less than humans, can aim toward spirituality. A motivation toward spirituality can be substituted for a motivation toward mere efficiency. Or, alternatively, a motivation toward an element of spirituality can be substituted. Essay 17 speaks of the substitution of love as a motivation, for instance. It is explained that the aiming is toward spirituality, or love, as a regulative ideal. That is, it is a standard toward which one aims, and it is a standard that one does not expect always to achieve.

The idea of bureaucracies and corporations aiming toward spirituality sounds less odd if it is conceptualized as operating as a subtext within an institution dominated by a major text of, say, making a profit. Alternatively, spirituality can be conceptualized as a major text, and profit-making can be a subtext. Further, spirituality is not a new aim. Such institutions as the Society of Jesus or the Dominicans—two Catholic religious orders—have always had quite definite spiritual aspirations, although their notion of spirituality is religious. Some educational institutions are well known as having the spiritual as part of their mission.

A vendor code of ethics provides another example of a business enterprise aiming toward greater spirituality and toward what the business deems to be "better" behavior. *Street Sense* is the publication of an organization for Washington, D.C.,'s poor and homeless. A few of the ten rules are:

> I agree to treat all others—customers, staff and other vendors—respectfully. I will not sell *Street Sense* under the influence of drugs and alcohol. I understand that *Street Sense* strives to be a self-sustaining paper that covers homelessness and poverty issues while providing a source of money for the homeless. As a result, I will try to help in this effort and spread the word. (*Street Sense,* March 15, 2004, 20)

Searching for spirituality through greater openness to the self is neither easy nor safe. It's not easy because, for one thing, ideas will differ about what searching means for an individual and for a bureaucracy or corporation. The organizational and procedural approaches will be different, of course. Public bureaucracies might require organizational arrangements parallel, say, to inspectors-general; individuals would not. For another thing, there are difficulties even in talking about the self, and some were discussed in Essay 3. The meaning of *self* is not at all straightforward. In my own case, I notice that I can look inside and see properties but I'm not sure if I can see my *self*. For another, human selves—and bureaucratic selves—are socially constructed. The autonomy of the "self" is also a contested topic. Recall, for example, how Nietzsche (1989, 24) points out that " . . . a thought comes when it wishes, and not when 'I' wish, so that it is a falsification of the facts of the case to say that the subject 'I' is the condition of the predicate 'think'."

Also searching-within is not safe. Sorry Immanuel Kant! The searcher-within might find the moral law, when morality even might not be a matter that should be conceptualized as "law." She might have seen what she wanted to see, and I think that Freud, Jung, and Lacan would hasten to agree. It's a more obvious safety matter when a Jim Jones looks inside himself and decides that all his followers should go to heaven by drinking poisoned Kool-Aid.

Style

Individuals and agencies, both public and private, in their justice-seeking should contemplate the style that they want for the construction of values. Searching-within isn't merely hunting through the attic of the mind to come up with—eureka!—hidden truths about values.

Function of Style

The concept of style moves toward center stage in postmetaphysical philosophy. Style was emphasized by Nietzsche, and it has been important for thinkers like Wittgenstein, Derrida, Foucault, and Gadamer, who appreciate the significance of context in philosophizing. It has been discussed by others like Nelson Goodman. Yet philosophical claims, including justice claims, are often made without conscious awareness of style.

The function of style is the creation of values. Nietzsche is the source of this claim, and I think it is useful for justice as seeking-within. It is the sense of style used under the next heading, *Choice of Style*. Nietzsche holds that style is necessary for characteristics like taste and for satisfaction—and thus for the ordering and construction of values. For example, he claims that a set of values grounded on a style that depicts life as God-given is a "declining, debilitated, weary, condemned life" (1968, 45). Nietzsche (1968, 47–54) goes on to explain that a set of values exhibits a different and robust style, for example, when that set of values presupposes a conceptualization of humans as people capable of living both with our mortality and without the prop of constructing a divinity. Style, for Nietzsche, is the ordering of preferences that constructs the person.

Nelson Goodman's view, although less expansive, is also useful for justice-as-seeking. Goodman rejects the received opinion that style can be understood as depending on an artist's conscious choice among alternative forms of expression. The received opinion is that style is an alternative way of saying synonymous things. Goodman rejects misleading oppositions between style and subject, form and content, and intrinsic and extrinsic features. Content and style are indeed interembedded (e.g., Goodman, 1978, 23); the content of justice claims and the style of such claiming are interrelated. Style is no less significant for the output of philosophizing than for the output of the artist.

On this view, not only the *what* (the content of a justice claim) but also the *how* (the way the claim is developed and made) should receive attention. So, whether to recognize (or ignore) justice style can be seen as a matter of the content of justice. We would say, for example, that evaluating whether or not to adopt a style of imposing the content of one's view of justice from a power position, backed by military or economic power, involves considerations of justice content. To do otherwise is to neglect the (in)justice of the unarticulated justice style.

Some philosophizing appeals to style or ultimate preferences, even when the appeal is unacknowledged. So we find the distinguished philosopher J.J. Smart renouncing any attempt to "prove" the act-utilitarian system that he advocates. He explains that some ethical disagreements depend simply on differences in ultimate preferences ("within the fields of personal decision, persuasion, advice and propaganda, but not within the field of academic philosophy"), although he does add that it is important to prevent this trend "from going too far" (Smart & Williams, 1973, 3).

Choice of Style

Postconventional justice is what I favor, although I don't see it in the same way that Lawrence Kohlberg does. Most are familiar with

Kohlberg's stages of moral development, and many are even more aware of the serious criticisms that have been advanced against his idea. They are aware of alternative schemes like Carol Gilligan's (1982) description of stages of care. Kohlberg speaks of nine stages, falling into the three broad categories of preconventional, conventional, and postconventional.

The highest category of postconventional morality, for Kohlberg, is that of universal principles and the demands of individual conscience. For him, a lower level of postconventional morality speaks of the social contract and individual rights. My emphasis here on style is similar to his emphasis in the highest category of post-conventional morality on individual input, modeling itself on the individual and imaginative creativity of philosophers like Kant and John Rawls and on moral leaders like Mahatma Gandhi (see quote above) and Martin Luther King. It is a view that can go against conventional or societal values. I do think that searching-within is facilitated if use is made of the justice arrangements discussed in Essays 11 and 12. Yet I don't think that Kohlberg is right that it *all* boils down to a matter of the cognition of universal principles— knowing principles that constitute systems of justice.

Nietzsche admired Jesus' moral creativity and despised the herd mentality of the Christians. Without being embroiled in that remark, I admire the moral creativity of people like Kohlberg, Gilligan— and even more that of Gandhi and King. Public bureaucracies typically are at one of the conventional stages. For both bureaucracies and selves, my preference is that style should reach up to the postconventional.

Seeking within my self could be facilitated by thinking in terms of a rough device to "measure" my style. Thermometer-like, it could ascend from the colder end that represents repression or denial of self, where the origins of my justice values are unknown even to me. It is a point where I make no attempt to find out what I *really* desire; it is where I make no attempt to tweak out the normative from within lived experiences. I could remain basically childlike, for example, simply inheriting the attitudes of my parents, my group, or my tribe. I could remain trapped within the "bureaucratic" limits of living, enthusiastically yet unthinkingly swallowing—hook, line, and sinker—some ethical, religious, or other bait "out there." The top of the warmer end would mark a style that emanates from complete self-actualization of "I" in all my lived dimensions. That is, it involves me—having overcome my self—in my biological, psychological, social, spiritual, and other dimensions.

My justice-seeking within the fiery depths would be higher on this thermometer-like scale than such seeking on the thin crust of lava. This is a reference to Bertrand Russell's meetings with Joseph Conrad and D.H. Lawrence. Russell shared with Conrad a belief that there is a difference between thinking and writing as "a dangerous walk on a thin crust of lava" and another level of writing where the writer sinks into the fiery depths, the "central fire" (Monk, 1996, 318). He shared with Lawrence the idea that writing should attempt to escape the prison, the hard shell that must be broken (Monk, 1996, 403).

Helping me ascend higher on the thermometer-like scale, as suggested before, is the idea of justice philosophizing going beyond disciplinary boundaries. It should go beyond, for example, to literature—and to psychoanalysis and more. What insights can I gain in my openness to my self by reflecting on the characters of Hamlet, Falstaff, Lady Macbeth, and even Titus Andronicus, for example? Harold Bloom (1998, 402) writes of Hamlet as having "a mind so powerful that the most contrary attitudes, values, and judgments can co-exist within it coherently . . ."

Style of justice thinking toward the warmer end of style cannot be identified with mere unreflective yelling deep from within the huggermugger of my guts, like a kind of primal scream. Transcending my self can build on such yelling and such primal screaming, or not; but it is not the same. I can never expect to succeed in knowing my self or in transcending my self *completely*. To become what I can, I must attempt to overcome my psychological, physical, social, spiritual, and other defects. No small task!

Epilogue

> What do you suppose would satisfy the soul,
> except to walk free and own no superior?
>
> —*Walt Whitman*

10 • Other and Hesitation

Empathy for the other should include authentic hesitation in justice-claiming. This is suggested both for individuals and for organizations. Such hesitation can take such forms as empathy of silence or empathy of listening. Authentic hesitation is in a long tradition of neighboring ideas in political philosophy.

> He who hesitates is lost.
>
> —*Proverb*

> Haste is ever the parent of failure.
>
> —*Proverb*

"I knew that my God was bigger than his. I knew that my God was a real God, and that his god was an idol." The lieutenant general spoke without authentic hesitation, as the story is reported (Cooper, 2003). The lieutenant general was William G. Boykin, then U.S. deputy undersecretary of intelligence, and he was referring to a 1993 battle between the United States and a Muslim militia leader in Somalia. "Enemy is a guy named Satan." His claim was about the justice of a military action, justifying the relations between a person and the other. If the reader is willing to view the military as a bureaucracy, it's a justice claim about the relations between a bureaucracy and the other. The point is not that the intelligence deputy undersecretary's claim is unintelligent, although the White House was prompted to issue a statement that the United States is not at war with Islam. Rather, the point is that General Boykin's claim was not made with authentic hesitation.

The more general point is about all justice claims, by individuals speaking for themselves, individuals speaking for public and private systems, and by public bureaucracies and private corporations themselves. In justice-seeking and practice, I suggest that every justice claim should be made with authentic hesitation about the claimant's own views and the views of her group or tribe or bureaucratic system. It is a minimal step toward what Jean-Jacques Rousseau calls a sociability of civility.

Authentic hesitation is a transforming, not a trivial, idea for governance. The first section of this essay describes minimal and more fulsome forms of authentic hesitation in making my own justice claims and in endorsing the claims of my group.

In the second section, I indicate how the impulses underlying "hesitation in claiming" have a long and broad history of neighboring antecedents in Western political philosophy, including recognition and respect. Although assertiveness has been privileged, there has been—as a sort of subtext—discussion of general virtues, trust, tolerance, sympathy, public reason, full consideration to the arguments of others, and more. Advocates have included Thomas Hobbes, John Locke, Georg Hegel, Adam Smith, Immanuel Kant, and John Rawls.

Authentic Hesitation

Authentic hesitation stands against an arrogant "I know best" or "my system is right" attitude on the part of governing bureaucracies and persons in power. It is required if claims are to be made justly by any bureaucrat, any businessperson, any individual, any politician, any judge. Anybody! Yet, I should reemphasize that authentic hesitation does not entail denying one's own beliefs. If a claimant genuinely believes that St. Augustine is right that true justice must take account of man's relations with God as well as relations between people and if that claimant believes that the claim should be made, for example, he should hold that view.

There are varieties of expressing empathy for the other. Among the range of alternatives, I want to point to a minimal form and a more fulsome form. By minimal, I mean a pause, an empathy of silence. This does include, of course, restraint in imposing my beliefs, through such acts as trickery or phony rhetoric—the kind of actions that are now standard in "good" business practice. It does include restraint in asserting my position and brooking no contrary position. It does exclude what Lieutenant General Boykin is reported to have done. But the minimal form can be conceptualized as authentic hesitation that grants a "minimal" space for the contrary views of others. A more fulsome form or level of authentic hesitation is what constitutes empathy of listening in genuine openness to the other. When United Nations and United States officials heard pleas to act against the massacres of Tutsis in Rwanda, empathy of listening would require genuine openness, for example, not focusing primarily on one's own concerns such as avoiding the spectacle of another Somalia debacle. The more fulsome form involves genuine listening (an idea evocative of anti-administration discussed in Essay 2) both to the mainstream and to the marginalized, like women, minorities, those with policed sexualities, foreigners, criminals, and outcasts.

Some readers will want to conceptualize hesitation by picturing it in terms of the response time between stimulus and response. They will note that some respondents are so hesitant that they are inclined either to act not at all (to complete inaction) or only when they are required to do so (only to necessary action); their response time is long. Somewhere near this end of the spectrum might be members in the (facetious) Society of Procrastinators; it is said that the society can take a decade or two before replying to membership applications. At the other end of the same "response time" spectrum are other people famous for their impetuosity. Some act on impulse, doing the first thing that comes into their heads. Between these two extremes are various intermediate dispositions, each shading into one another. The kind of hesitation we are speaking of is not psychological or motor, however; it is ethical. Authentic hesitation does not mean endorsing inauthentic hesitation, which can be a matter of mere procrastination—a putting off of what can be said and done. Authentic hesitation should be motivated by either moral principle, moral impulse, *or* conscience. Principled hesitation can be connected with the word "scruples," coming from the Old French *scruple* and the Latin *scrupulus*. The Latin *scrupulus* literally means a sharp stone or pebble.

This talk of authentic hesitation is intended to apply to the justice-seeking and practice of public and private organizations no less than to individuals. Arguably, this would constitute a sea change in the culture of organizations. Like private, public bureaucracies have a well-known disposition to cover themselves, including lying and organization-speak. This has been intensified in recent years by public relations and related activities. Look at the newspapers; listen to the news. Story after story appears showing public and private organizations saying that they are right, when they know that they are wrong. Then there are the "good" business practices mentioned earlier, like trickery and half truths in advertising.

All categories of moral propositions justifying action deserve authentic hesitation, in my view. But I can imagine some wanting hesitation applied differentially, that is, wanting more hesitancy about some things than others. They might construct a typology based on social utility (e.g., propositions it is essential for the masses to believe, those desirable for them to believe, and indifferent propositions) or based on age (e.g., exempting children from unpleasantness). In thinking this through, however, recall that there is a difference between action and justifying action.

An argument for authentic hesitation in governance can be presented in terms of Foucault's claim that we should recognize the "fascism in us all." Foucault (1977, viii) asks, "How do we ferret out the fascism that is ingrained in our behavior?" Elsewhere I (1995) have suggested that this tendency should be recognized as a hazard of being a manager.

Another argument is from our epistemological limitations. Questioning the leading spirits of his day in the bright light of the marketplace, Plato's Socrates was one who recognized such limitations. He would question General Laches, represented as a character in Plato's dialog of the same title, for example. He disquieted the general into recognition that Laches—the courageous general, exhorting others to courage in the face of death—could not give a coherent account of courage.

On this second line of argument, I notice that most of what I internalized about justice was at my grandmother Eva's knee or in kindergarten—when I was not in a good position to make critical judgments. Or, you and I learned to hate injustice when, as children, we witnessed a helpless nerd-child being chased mercilessly by the local bully. Or, we learned to imagine love when we melted at the gaze of a local belle. Much of the rest that we "know" about justice comes from (nothing against grandmothers, bullies, and belles) sources with axes to grind. Much comes from the self-interest of our group and other groups—our gender, economic, social, national, or other classes. Much comes from the self-interest of powerful forces in society. Thrasymachus in Plato's *Republic* was right, and he was right to be angry about it. Much in justice is what is in the interest of the stronger. Much in a sense of justice depends on accident. Much that we count as justice understanding (see Essay 7) is our justice legacy, swallowed whole.

Yet, symbolic systems can favor *action now*. Hesitation is marginalized in the English language, for instance. The synonyms and near-synonyms for hesitation suggest a tale. Synonyms for hesitating include vacillating, procrastinating, and faltering. More synonyms and near-synonyms of "to hesitate" include to "hold back; be dubious; be uncertain; flounder; straddle; stay one's hand; change one's mind; trim; shy at; seesaw back and forth; not know what to do; be irresolute; pull back; waver; dawdle; oscillate; tergiversate; turn one's back on; shrink; equivocate; drag one's feet; hang off; hem and haw; blow hot and cold; dillydally; straddle the fence; leave up in the air; make bones about; do figure eights; flinch; shy away from; not face up to; let something slide; hang fire; wait to see how the wind blows; wrinkle one's brow; be irresolute; make a difficulty; hide one's head in the sand; and wait to see how the cat jumps. The list goes on.

Society in general can favor *action now*. Hesitation is marginalized in societies fixated on winning, on being number one. As just indicated, such attitudes are supported by—and reflected in—symbolic systems. Aren't there more antihesitation than prohesitation proverbs and sayings? "She who hesitates is lost." Even American baseball penalizes a pitcher for balking, for hesitating.

Neighboring Antecedents

There is a broad and long history of neighboring antecedents of hesitation. Examples of these antecedent concepts are the *general civic virtues,* the particular virtues of *trust, tolerance, mutual respect, mutual recognition, sympathy,* virtues required in *public reason,* and those involved in giving *full consideration to the arguments of others.* I call them antecedents because these concepts preceded authentic hesitation. These antecedents are neighboring in that they share the view that a successful society requires a certain restraint from "preferred" behavior, a curbing of self-interested or other "natural" behavior.

Features could be added from organizational thinking. Being open to subordinates and being open to customers, for instance, exhibit kinds of hesitation.

General Virtues

Start with the example of general virtues as a neighboring antecedent of hesitation. The variety of virtues that have been considered necessary for a successful society includes what William Galston calls the "general virtues," like willingness to obey laws and a sense of loyalty to society's basic political institutions and principles (Galston, 1991). There are civic virtues required for economic growth. With the collapse of communism, for example, there has been increasing concern in Eastern Europe and elsewhere with the cultural characteristics that are desirable for such growth. The work ethic, doing one's job well, supporting oneself, and openness to economic change are examples.

Trust

Trust is another neighbor of hesitation, in that attitudes like confidence and reciprocal courtesy are involved in being hesitant about one's own justice assertions. However, trust is also compatible with nonhesitancy. Some describe "trust" as a public good supplied in the past by traditional structures like religion; they now suppose that, with the erosion of these structures, this trust should be supplied by other elements in civil society (e.g., Seligman, 1992). Trust is said to be necessary for the functioning of a society through a range of situations, including the making of economic and other agreements and promises. "Trust, the capacity to commit oneself to fulfilling the legitimate expectations of others, is both the constitutive virtue of, and the key precondition for the existence of, any society" (Dunn, 1984, 287). Appeals are made to the role of trust in thinkers like Hobbes, Locke, Tocqueville, and others. As Tocqueville writes, "Each man having some right and being sure of the enjoyment of those rights, there would be established between all classes a manly [*sic*] confidence and a sort of reciprocal courtesy, as far removed from pride as from servility" (Tocqueville, 1999, 12).

Toleration

Toleration is highly valued in classical liberalism. John Locke's religious toleration, for instance, extends to not interfering with the religious practices of others. It is an attitude developed within the context of Locke's other views, that individuals must observe certain constraints in pursuing their self-identified interests, and these constraints constitute the civic virtues that protect the rights and liberties of all. So, for example, no one is to harm another; in fact, we are to preserve the "life, the liberty, health, limb, or goods of another" as long as our own preservation is not at issue (Locke, 1988, 271). Individuals are constrained in such areas as permitting property rights and the rule of the constrained majority, as another example. So Locke's *Letter on Toleration* claims that all people are free to believe as they wish, as long as they do not deny basic rights to others. Locke's view denies toleration to atheists, however; it also leaves Catholics and agnostics in a dubious position.

Mutual Respect

Mutual respect is a virtue that demands more than the live-and-let-live attitude of toleration. It is a civic virtue that has a role in such thinkers as Hobbes, Hegel, Mill, and Rawls. Hobbes's laws of nature, governing conduct in society, can be understood as suggesting mutual respect. Hobbes holds that these laws of nature are "contrary to our naturall [*sic*] Passions, that carry us to partiality, Pride, Revenge, and the like" and they need the "terrour of some Power to cause them to be observed" (Hobbes, 1991, 117).

Mutual Recognition

Mutual recognition is a type of mutual respect. Hegel's concept of mutual recognition and his commitment to public discourse founded in an ethical state expect that people pay heed to one another within the political process. Mutual respect is required for each to be fully human, as discussed in Hegel's celebrated dialectic of the master and the slave.

Sympathy

We find Adam Smith writing of the propensity to sympathize with others. For him, economic life should be seen against a larger background of natural sympathy. The bulk of Smith's *Theory of Moral Sentiments* is concerned with moral psychology; the last seventh of the book deals with moral philosophy. The book can be seen as a discussion of how human beings, self-serving as they are, are able to create natural impediments against the inclinations of their own passions. Sympathy, a fellow feeling for the other person "at the thought of his situation," is at the heart of Smith's moral psychology. Sympathy is the basis of our judgments about the propriety and merit of the conduct of others. Looking at one's own behavior as if one were another person allows one to evaluate one's own conduct. We can identify the general rules that govern conduct and give rise to our sympathy. Smith's moral philosophy discussed the nature and basis of virtue. For Smith there is no single criterion of virtue; it gives scope to propriety, prudence, and benevolence. Neither prudence (seeking self-interest) nor benevolence (seeking others' interests) is enough by itself. In this circumstance, the standard of what is appropriate behavior is given in considering impartial sympathetic feelings. Sympathy (for Smith) is the test of morality, the sympathy of the impartial and well-informed spectator.

Public Reason

Mutual respect in Immanuel Kant is further developed in terms of the notion of public reason, whereby individuals show mutual respect in critical thinking that takes into account the views of others. Three rules should be followed in this process. Each person should think for herself, free from superstition and "self-incurred tutelage" (Kant, 1957, 3). Each person should seek "enlarged thought"—establishing with others a common and universal viewpoint for evaluating views and pursuing the truth. Each person should "think consistently" (Kant, 1957, 136–137). The motivation for such public reasoning may be found in Kant's categorical imperative. As mentioned in Essay 3, the imperative requires that individuals should treat each person as an end and not as a means only. A ticket clerk is not merely a means to my obtaining a ticket, for instance; a voter is not merely a means to a politician obtaining a vote; and so on. Public reason as a concept was democratized more fully by writers like Mill and Rawls than in Kant's account; Hegel also wrote about public reason. Kant's own view is that public reason, requiring a scholarly perspective, would be limited to those who have an independent position. People like domestic servants, women, and apprentices would be excluded. For Hegel, it occurred mainly between the monarch and the legislature.

Full Consideration of the Arguments of Others

Committed to free and open discussion, John Stuart Mill argues that open discourse and intellectual flourishing require giving full consideration to the arguments of others (Mill, 1961). He claims that we must not suppress opinions. His argument is that experience is not enough as a guide to life; rather, "there must be discussion, to show how experience is to be interpreted" (Mill, 1961, 205). "Checking an opinion against those of others is the only stable foundation for a just reliance on it" (Mill, 1961, 209). Mill goes on to say that knowing what can be said against any claim and having opposed all opponents, "He has a right to think his judgment better than that of any person, or any multitude, who has not gone through a similar process" (Mill, 1961, 209). Rawls adopts Kant's approach to public reason. He thinks that public reasoning should take place within "a political conception of justice based on the values that the others can reasonably be expected to endorse" (Rawls, 1993, 226). His guidelines provide that we should use approaches to reasoning found not only in science but also in common sense. They also provide that there should be an open discussion of public issues. There must be a commitment to civility. Also (a strange claim), people should not use a particular nonpublic religion or philosophical position as a basis for a basic justice claim.

Other Examples

There is a large literature on other values needed in communities. For example, it is argued that values should include a reflective politics of self-control and self-limitation (Offe et al., 1991). Other suggestions include decency (Margalit, 1996) and identification with the constitutive institutions and practices (Dauenhauer, 1996).

Epilogue

> Ballpoint pens will not work in 0 gravity. NASA scientists (unhesitantly?) spent a decade and $12 billion developing a pen that writes in zero gravity, upside down, underwater, on almost any surface including glass and at temperatures ranging from below freezing to over 300° centigrade. The Russians used a pencil.

> —*Provided by Judith Twigg, 2003*

11 • Tradition: Golden Ruling

Traditional insights, when open-ended, facilitate justice as seeking wisdom. The Golden Rule is discussed as an example. It is popular, but ignored by most modern philosophers. It emphasizes the "I" in determining the relationship of governance to the other and to the expanding sphere of altruism.

> Do to others, as you would that they do to you.
>
> —*Golden Rule*

Individuals and officials should seek justice wisdom in, among other places, traditional insights that are open-ended. I imagine governance officials encouraged to contemplate and to dialogue about such justice insights, with all the earnestness that is now devoted to examining the technical aspects of programs. I imagine a quantum upgrading of bureaucratic eth-talk and eth-practice, exploring within the constraining framework of laws.

Justice-seeking should turn to the wisdom available, among other sources, from tradition. A motive in including this essay and the next is to emphasize that justice-seeking within my self and my relation-to-the-other (see Essays 9 and 10) can be shallow if it is attempted in an intellectual vacuum. It is not a task merely for chat in a hot tub. But recommended insights are those that are open-ended.

By justice insights that are open-ended, I mean formulations of regulative ideals, first, that are conducive to the practice of justice-seeking and, second, that do not privilege closure. First, formulations are open-ended in encouraging radical justice creativity, fostering the justice imagination of *I* in relation to the *other.* They are, in a sense, gnostic. Second, the formulations are incomplete as decision systems in that they do not offer a watertight ethical prescription. They are tolerant, as it were, of aporia.

I wondered about borrowing a word for this kind of ethical insight that is open-ended. *Arrangement* would have been suitable in the sense described in Essay 13. *Koan* refers to a riddle which has no answer but which leads to enlightenment. But it is not suitable, because the open-ended insights are not riddles without answers.

Let's proceed by example—an example of a traditional justice insight that is open-ended. The first section of this essay speaks of the Golden Rule jingle—or principle, prescription, proverb, adage, precept, bumper sticker, or one-liner. It turns to what I think is a lacuna in inherited justice thinking. The second section speaks to the open-endedness of the Golden Rule. It suggests how the rule encourages the moral creativity of the "I" in shaping an individual's—and a bureaucracy's—relationship to the *other.*

Golden Rule Jingle

Question: What traditional justice insight (a) has enjoyed widespread popularity throughout much of the World and throughout much of recorded history and (b) has been essentially dismissed by modern philosophers? Answer: The Golden Rule jingle; *I* should choose to act toward others in the same way as *I* think that they should (ought to) act toward me.

Turn to this puzzle about the Golden Rule, noticing the promised lacuna or Freudian slip in the structure of our inherited justice philosophy.

First Horn

Turn to the first horn of the puzzle, item (a) that asks about the Rule's popularity. The Golden Rule principle, minus the name or term, is ancient and unusually widely acknowledged. The name itself is relatively modern; the first use of the term may be in Edward Gibbon's *The History of the Decline and Fall of the Roman Empire,* published between 1776 and 1788. The Golden Rule principle itself is prominent in important religions. It is present in Christianity, Judaism, Confucianism, Buddhism, Zoroastrianism, and in Hinduism.

The Golden Rule principle is not confined to religions, however. It is widely recognized in popular cultures, as in those of ancient Greece and ancient Rome. It is true that enthusiasts have overclaimed in attempting to demonstrate the *almost universal* appeal of the rule. There is a difference between being a central element in an ethical tradition and being peripheral. The mere mention of an item in a text does not entail that item's importance, for example. The fact remains, however, that the Golden Rule principle long has been widely accepted, including acceptance by many of our contemporaries who have never thought it through.

The Second Horn

The second horn of the puzzle—item (b) about "unpopularity"— is that the Golden Rule has been essentially dismissed by modern philosophers. This is not to deny that philosophers have had important things to say about the Golden Rule. They certainly have, including thinkers like Hobbes, Leibniz, Spinoza, Locke, Reid, Paine, Kant, Schopenhauer, and Mill. Even a few—very few— recent and contemporary philosophers have discussed the Golden Rule, like Peter Singer and Allen Gewirth. Yet, the Golden Rule has received short shrift from modern philosophers. This claim has been noticed by others. For example, Gould (1963, 10) says, "As an ethical standard, the Golden Rule is not highly thought of by philosophers writing in the area of ethics. They seldom mention it." Singer (1967, 365) can also write that the "Golden Rule has been the subject of comparatively little philosophical discussion. It is usually mentioned, when it is mentioned at all, only in passing. . . ." In moral and social philosophy, the jingle of the Golden Rule is faint.

The Leibnizian-Kantian criticism is the major reason for the Rule's neglect. The criticism is that the Golden Rule offers no standard or criterion of right action. Leibniz writes that the Golden Rule, although it shows a way to acquire such a standard, presupposes a standard of conduct. If I am a convinced corrupt politician, for example, the Golden Rule by itself will not encourage me to end my corrupt practices. It will encourage me to deal with the *other* no worse than I want to be dealt with myself. Immanuel Kant emphasized his view that the Golden Rule contains nothing about duties to others, and nothing about duties to oneself. He wrote, "Let it not be thought that the common [Golden Rule] could serve here as the rule or principle of duties to oneself, nor of the duties of benevolence to others (for many a one would gladly consent that others should not benefit him, provided only that they might be excused from showing benevolence to them) nor finally that of duties of strict obligation to one another. . . ." (Kant, 1950, 88). Hans Reiner (1983, 274–275) is right in commenting that "Kant succeeded with his objections almost in invalidating the Golden Rule and in disqualifying it from future discussion in ethics. Among Continental European philosophers after Kant only Schopenhauer has attached a high value to it."

All the criticisms relate to the fact that the Golden Rule is a "rule" that is not really a rule. These criticisms are cogent, in my opinion, only if the need is for a definitive and complete system for determining what should be. Anything less is unacceptable to those who want a single adage to yield the final answer. The Golden Rule does not provide the kind of complete and definitive decision rule that Leibniz and Kant think they need. Yet this is the lacuna or Freudian slip in a discipline that can be described as exhibiting no progressivity (see Essay 8). The lacuna is in shutting out the option that, if anything else normative is needed from the Golden Rule, the rest must come from justice-seeking within me.

The Other: Interpretation

It is in defining the *other*, no less than the *I*, that the Golden Rule stimulates justice-as-seeking. The *other* in the jingle could extend to all humans, or I could create levels of *other* by limiting that application to a subset, such as my friends, my tribe, my ethnic group, my economic class, my peers in the bureaucracy, my bureaucracy, my corporation, my board of directors, my nation, my gender. I think that the sphere should extend to all persons; but not all do. Encouraged by the open-ended nature of the Golden Rule, the creativity of justice-seeking should turn to the context of the expanding circle of altruism.

The circle of altruism has expanded over the millennia beyond the particular group, as Peter Singer explains. This circle refers to the range of application for the equal consideration of other humans and beyond. The circle limited to a particular group results in the kind of ethical thinking that can lead even Aristotle, discussing enslavement, to discriminate between barbarians and Greeks. The moral sphere or the circle of altruism has increasingly expanded to include all humans. The sphere has expanded so that it extends, for some, to other animals like dogs and cats. It has even expanded to trees and mountains, and beyond. Describing this expanding circle, Singer writes that the "shift from a point of view that is disinterested between individuals within a group, but not between groups, to the point of view that is fully universal, is a tremendous change—so tremendous, in fact, that it is only just beginning to be accepted on the level of ethical reasoning . . . Nevertheless, it is the direction in which moral thought has been going since ancient times" (Singer, 1981, 113).

It is *as if* we have been inching through stages from pack animal through polis-worshiper to a postpolis context. In this *as if* evolutionary moral process, often we yearn for the comforts of the previous stage. Each succeeding stage seems to require more from us in terms of our inner resources—from our imaginative and other psychic energies.

More elaborate accounts are available, equally deconstructible yet perhaps more satisfying. A hint of the complexity is given in Eibl-Eibesfeldt's comment (1982, 6) that people were "originally created for a life in individualized groups. The transition to life in the anonymous community produces problems of identification. On the one hand the urge clearly exists to form a bond with strangers as well. On the other hand we can observe the inclination to cut oneself off in groups from others."

For the first stage of this appearance of an evolutionary moral process, let's appeal to a natural history of human behavior patterns and to the pack behavior of the human. As Eibl-Eibesfeldt points out (1982, 75), "Many features of our human territorial behavior point to our ancient primate heritage. . . . Human beings defend both individual territories (including personal property) and group territories. In addition, every individual shows the unmistakable tendency to keep his distance from strangers, except in special circumstances (buses, mass meetings)." Is it too strong to describe humans in terms of pack animals? Pack animals have different ways of "knowing their own." Rats mark one another, as Eibl-Eibesfeldt tells us, to create a common scent group. If a rat is removed from the pack for a few days, it will be attacked when it is returned to the pack because it has lost its smell. An alien or immigrant rat smeared with the proper urine will be accepted. Processed through a urinary melting pot, the alien is an okay rat.

For the second stage, let's enlist Thomas Jefferson in appealing to the ancient Greeks and to Aristotle in particular. Jefferson and the Founding Fathers looked back with admiration and with a kind of love as they tried in important part to re-create on a continental scale the kind of Greek polis that they admired. The polis, the city-state or country, is the means through which humans can achieve the good life. In his celebrated phrase, Aristotle said that man is a political animal. By this, he meant that it is not possible to be fully human except through active participation in the political, through life in the system of the polis that functions—as it were—as a moral "church." The polis, the perfect association that exists by nature, is logically prior to the individual. A human and a polis can be compared to a hand (or foot) and a body. The hand cannot be a real hand without the body; so a man cannot be fully human without the polis. In his equally celebrated phrase, Aristotle wrote that a person who can live outside the polis is either a god or a beast, subhuman or a superhuman (Barker, 1958, 6).

For a postpolis stage of moral globalism, significant arguments are advanced by writers like Michael Ignatieff and (again) Peter Singer. Ignatieff (1984, 139) holds that "A century of total war has taught us where belonging can take us when its object is the nation." He prefers that our human needs, our sense of belonging, should instead center on "a new form, a new kind of object: the fragile green and blue earth itself, the floating disk we are the first generation to see from space" (Ignatieff, 1984, 139).

The Golden Rule and the expanding circle of altruism raise the question whether governance should not design arrangements with a sphere of application such that all humans are treated with equal consideration for their interests. It is the question of how the *other* should be interpreted in the Golden Rule. Such justice-seeking questions are raised in a situation where governance thinking and practice is frozen in large part within the polis stage. On the one hand, this is an age of the international corporation, and economic theory in principle is not limited by national boundaries. Capitalism wants to extend throughout the world, and largely has. Democracy has similar aspirations, and in a variety of forms it is a widely used system. There are area studies in political science, and there is comparative public administration. On the other hand, there is the parochialism. For example, why is Woodrow Wilson the father of the public administration that is studied in the United States? Why is political theory so subservient to the Western philosophical canon? Why are international politics so dominated by national self-interest? And so on.

For my money, the Golden Rule suggests that governance should not confine the ethical sphere to particular classes of people, like males or the dominant economic group. Justice-as-seeking should go beyond such limits as the customer and the client, beyond the good citizen. The *I* should shift toward equal consideration of the interests of all humans, including humans beyond the limits of national boundaries. For the postpolis stage, I am not *advocating* that the nation-state system should disappear—although it is being modified even now. Rather, it's a matter of our symbolic and moral relationships toward nationality. As this interpretation of the Golden Rule implies, polis-worship should wither.

12 • Other Traditions: Silver Ruling

Seeking justice wisdom from literatures in other cultural traditions should be the rule rather than the exception. As an example, contrast Confucianism and Christianity in their attitudes toward hesitancy and assertiveness.

> The man of perfect virtue is cautious and
> slow in his speech.
>
> —*Confucius*

Seek justice wisdom from the literatures of other cultural traditions, routinely! The conversation of humankind that Michael Oakeshott describes is not Western property. The seedbed of justice wisdom is not as narrowly Western as is—shame on it!—our inheritance of disciplinary moral philosophy. Why hasn't this extension to other cultures happened more in ethics? There have been exceptions. Schopenhauer and Heidegger, philosophers, are examples. My suggestion is that seeking justice wisdom from all cultural traditions should be the rule.

This essay underlines this suggestion about seeking justice wisdom. There is much to learn about justice from foreign traditions. Two caveats. First, I don't want to suggest that the dominant attitudes of cultures or civilizations are fixed, invariant, or uniform. Nor do I want to say that each individual's thinking is a reflection only of her culture. That would be a mistake (Said, 1978). Second, rather than focusing on cultures, justice-seeking might instead concentrate on individuals. Mahatma Gandhi was a well-known practitioner of nonviolent disobedience, a kind of authentic hesitation (see Essay 10). Emperor Chin was not.

Regulative ethical ideals are achieved only irregularly, typically. Look at European, American, Japanese, or Chinese history for similar catalogs of much beauty and much violent brutality. Nevertheless, I want to suggest that a difference can be drawn between regulative ethical ideals or traditions in populations affected by Confucianism and populations impacted by Christianity. I want to contrast what, for their founders and adherents, are central justice ideals—the Silver Rule and The Golden Rule.

Expressed by Confucius and thus culturally and politically associated with the set of populations that Confucianism affected, the Silver Rule is "Do not do to others as they should not do to you." The Golden Rule, expressed by Christ (and by Lao-tze) and thus culturally and politically associated with another affected set of populations, is "Do to others as they should do to you."

The Silver Rule (the negative form, as the Christians put it) and the Golden Rule (the positive form) are logically equivalent. They are equivalent in the sense that a want, wish, or desire expressed in negative terms can always be reformulated in positive terms. There is no difference between a person not wanting others to lie to her and wanting them not to lie to her; and "A wants Y to occur" is equivalent to "A does not want Y not to occur." Yet the connotations are quite different. There are rhetorical and psychological distinctions; there is a marked difference in emphasis. Just as there is no logical deduction from either of the rules to either hesitation or assertiveness, so the difference in connotation does not "entail" one or the other result. Yet a result in the difference in connotation is that there is a ready association between the Confucian Silver Rule and hesitation, and conversely in the relation between the positive Christian form and assertiveness.

Consider first the centrality of the Silver Rule and then hesitancy in Confucian ethics. Central in Confucian philosophy are the notions of *jen* and *shu*, the latter being the procedure for practicing *jen*. *Jen* has been variously translated as perfect virtue, magnanimity, moral life, moral character, man-to-manness [*sic*], true manhood, and so on (e.g., see Oldstone-Moore, 2002). The Chinese character for *jen* is described as consisting of two parts, one signifying man and the other meaning many or society. We read about *shu* in the *Analects of Confucius,* the Confucian "Bible" written some seventy years after Confucius's death, which may have been in the year 479 B.C. It reads, "Tzu-kung asked, 'Is there a single word which can be a guide to conduct throughout life?' The Master said, 'It is perhaps the word "shu." Do not impose on others what you yourself do not desire." In another place Tseng-tzu adds to Confucius's comment that there is a single thread binding his way together, saying that, "The way of the Master consists of chung and shu." *Chung* here may mean doing one's best. References to the Silver Rule occur elsewhere in the *Analects.* For example, in *Analects,* v. 11, Tzu-kung said, "What I do not wish man to do to me, I also wish not to do to men." To this Confucius replied, "Ah, Tz'u! That is beyond you" (Legge, 1960, 177).

Now turn to hesitancy. In Legge's translation, the *Analects* reads that "Sze-ma Niu asked about perfect virtue. The Master said, 'The man of perfect virtue is cautious and slow in his speech.' 'Cautious and slow in his speech!' said Niu, 'Is that what is meant by perfect virtue?' The Master said, 'When a man feels the difficulty of doing, can he be other than cautious and slow in speaking?'" (Legge, 1960, bk. 12, ch. 3). In Lau's translation, the same passage reads "Su-ma Niu asked about benevolence. The Master said, 'The mark of the benevolent man is that he is loath to speak.' 'In that case, can a man be said to be benevolent simply because he is loath to speak?' The Master said, 'When to act is difficult, is it any wonder that one is loath to speak?'" (Lau, 1979, bk. 12, ch. 3). Professor Sung Ho Chung believes that Legge's translation is better than Lau's, because he thinks that the original character should not be translated as "loath (or unwilling). It means a state of being patient, difficult, not easily speaking out, so cautious and slow" (Chung, 1997).

The place of hesitancy in Confucianism can be better appreciated by considering the intent of Confucianism. As Chung puts it, "Government officials are presupposed to be the major readers of the books. The main questions dealt with throughout the texts of Confucius and Mencius are such as: What is a human being? How should human beings live together in a society which needs organizations and leaders? How should leaders act and organizations be run? The word 'publicness' in contrast with individual 'selfish-ness' is one of the most important concepts explored throughout the philosophy. The major concern is how to avoid inhumaneness (or alienation) in bureaucratic society (the question we are still struggling to answer). The ideal state (or virtue) of a human being represented by the word 'jen' (perfect virtue or benevolence) in Confucianism, I think, means to be 'socially' perfect or benevo-lent" (Chung, 1997).

Associating hesitancy with Confucianism does not mean that assertiveness is excluded, either from practice or even as playing some role in the constitution of the ideal. It is a question of the relative emphasis or proportion between the opposing tendencies, and that is why it is desirable to write about "privileging hesitancy over assertiveness." The suggestion is not that either tendency is completely absent but that one tendency can be more or less domi-nant. This is reflected in Professor Chung's comment on Confu-cianism that, "I don't think any society in history has realized the Confucian philosophy in social and political practices as Confucius argues, even though we (East Asian countries) had a long history of regarding Confucianism as the dominant and official social philosophy. Philosophy was simply used for political purposes" (Chung 1997).

Consider now the role of the Golden Rule and the privileging of assertiveness over hesitation in the Christian tradition. The most celebrated statements of the positive rule occur in the New Testa-ment accounts of Matthew and Luke (7:12 and 6:31, respectively), and the commands for compliance, love of one's enemies, and the Golden Rule are described as pointing to the Q-source. "So what-soever you wish that men should do to you, do so to them" reads the former; "And as you wish that men would do to you, do so to them" reads the latter. The importance of the Golden Rule is sug-gested by the next line in Matthew, reading "for this is the law and the prophets." Paul Ricoeur interprets this as contrasting what he calls the logic of superabundance with the logic of equivalence, which governs everyday ethics and "which finds its perfect ex-pression in the Golden Rule" (Ricoeur, 1990, 392). The Golden Rule, even though it does occur in Christian texts in the negative

124 JUSTICE AS SEEKING

as well as in the positive form and despite such interpretations, has an important place in Christian ethics.

Like in the Confucian case, it is not an either-or situation; it is not suggested that either hesitancy or assertiveness are excluded. Rather, I repeat that it is a matter of one ideal or tendency being privileged over the other. So, some may well pick out an important hesitant subtheme in Christianity. They may point to the element of humility in the complex tradition. They might point, for example, to the injunction to turn the other cheek, to the stress on love and charity, to the unworldliness of many saints and ascetics, to the pacifism of groups like the Society of Friends, or even to the report of God's penultimate hesitation in dealing with Job.

Yet an unhesitant quality has been pervasive and dominant in Christianity, suggested by the notion of being a "soldier of Christ" and reflected in missionary zeal. Even in the early centuries before the religion was adopted by the Roman Empire and even while there was no interest among Christians in human justice issues and in secular reform (unimportant to early Christians who believed in the immanence of the "Kingdom of God"), there was among the non-gnostic mainstream no hesitation in belief and in proclaiming. This lack of hesitation was reflected in the Christian attitudes towards faith, conversion, and martyrdom. It would be reflected in later years in the attitude toward heretics and infidels. At one level of assertiveness, Christians were proud to be members of "the Church Militant" and looked forward to "the Church Triumphant." They saw themselves struggling with Satan, recollecting the original clash of assertiveness when God was described as ejecting from Heaven an archangel who asserted his own pride. At another level of aggressive assertiveness, there were the wars of the Crusades and the tortures of the Holy Inquisition.

The latter assertiveness is symbolized, for me, by the imprisonment and death in 1600 of Giordano Bruno. I have sat at a café table in the Campo dé Fiori (Field of Flowers) in Rome, near Bruno's statue. I have put flowers on the statue; they were filched within minutes, probably sensibly returned to the flower stands. Yellow daffodils! Bruno was a monk and a bold philosopher who had published his metaphysical views while he was "on the run" from church authorities. He took the position that matters of speculation in philosophy should be distinguished sharply from theological views; and on the latter he argued that he had been entirely orthodox. Bruno was unhesitant and assertive. The Inquisition was aggressive. There were seven years of imprisonment and torture in Venice and in Rome. The Inquisition declined Bruno the usual kindness of garroting him before the flames of the execution could engulf him. The Holy Inquisition burned Bruno to death, in the Field of Flowers.

III

Practice as Art

The man of system . . . is apt to be very wise in his own
conceit; and is often so enamored with the supposed
beauty of his own ideal plan of government, that he
cannot suffer the smallest deviation from any part of it.

—Adam Smith

What Is Post-Traditional Practice?

Post-traditional practice is art, and the practitioner is then artist.
These essays indicate constitutive features of post-traditional practice in terms of, symbolically, killing the king. Ideas and themes
that recur include machines, hierarchy of power, individual humans and, above all, resymbolization.

The first essay speaks of governance as machines. The next two
discuss power relations in traditional and nontraditional governance. The following two essays point to new parameters in macro
understanding and sensitivity in governance, and the final essay
analyzes opening democracy.

13 • Start with Michelangelo: What I, a Bureaucrat, Expect

Practitioners should be artists. Practice as art should include thinking as playing and justice as seeking. Beyond this, practice as art should engage the day-to-day with concern about the relationship between the totality of political, economic and administrative systems and the individual human. The art of governance should seek to kill the king. One face of the king is the view of governance as a matter of machine systems and technicism.

> When I told my father that I wished to be an artist,
> he flew into a rage, 'artists are laborers,
> no better than shoemakers.'
>
> —*Michelangelo Buonarroti*

The statue David is about governance and killing, and Michelangelo Buonarroti can be seen as about the level of artistry to which governance practice as art should aspire. Not an impossible dream! Sublime is the statue of David, which Michelangelo released from a nineteen-foot-tall block of damaged marble in 1504 and which is now surrounded by tourists in the Accademia in Italy's Florence. It was a governmental public relations job and a work of art.

Like Michelangelo, practitioners of governance should be artists in their practice. They should relish practice as art, which includes thinking as playing and justice as thinking. They should possess the knowledge, abilities, and skills (in the officialese of job specifications) required for this artistry. Some will wish to restrict this expectation, in a hierarchical democracy, to those toward the top of the pile. I don't.

Florence had recently been redeclared a republic, and it faced lethal enemies. Michelangelo's statue David represents Florence, city of David and seedbed of many David statues—like Donatello's bronze, which is my favorite. As Michelangelo writes in his diary, "A civic hero, [statue David] was a warning . . . whoever governed Florence should govern justly and defend it bravely. Eyes watchful . . . the neck of a bull . . . hands of a killer . . . the body a reservoir of energy. He stands poised to strike" (Bonner, 2004). Michelangelo carved a worried and tense look in and around the eyes of David engaged with the unseen enemy, Goliath. He sculpted elegance in the face and in the body. But there is the powerful hand grasping a stone in a sling. Michelangelo produced David the determined killer. In carrying out his public relations job for the city's wool guild in support of the government of Florence, Michelangelo is above all a committed artist, even if his father Ludovico—a minor government official—thinks that that is like being a shoemaker. Michelangelo created a work of art that is sublime and that can induce in onlookers a sense of the sublime. For us now well removed from the heat and danger of Renaissance Florence, the statue points to what is possible.

Like Michelangelo's David, the art of governance practice should aim to create in a way that implicates the sublime. I am using sublime in the ordinary sense of exceeding the merely beautiful and mere categorization. I mean the sublime that touches and enriches the humanity of humans that encounter it, or not! Even in a governmental system designed as a machine, the sublime can emerge once in a while in the individual poetic humanity of, say, a truly unusual president, a truly unusual corporate CEO, or a truly unusual postal worker. Meet Nelson Mandela; Fannie Lou Hamer; Winston Churchill; John F. Kennedy . . . It jumps out, and touches us. It emerges in Michelangelo's public relations statue. It should be the stock-in-trade of the post-traditional practitioner.

The post-traditional bureaucrat should do better than Michelangelo in confronting the machine, however. She should arm herself with a perspective that is greater than just "doing my job." She should have a larger intellectual perspective with which to confront the "necessities" of the day-to-day. This perspective centers on understandings such as that of the interrelationship of the totality of political, economic, and administrative sociotechnologies to the human individual. The keys are the *totality* and the *human individual*. She should engage the day-to-day with wisdom and concern about such interrelationships.

This series of essays (13 through 18) depicts critical features of practice as art. It looks toward practice as art that transforms everyday chores with the sublime. It is art that aims to kill the king. This essay describes one feature or, to use the royal image, one royal face. This feature or face is the view of governance as mere systems and technicism. It poses two questions about machine systems. The essay then turns to what I, as a bureaucrat, expect.

The Machine System

Most of us are relatively helpless in the face of the accelerating onrush of the totality of sociotechnology. We enthuse and yearn for more "stuff," and relatively few complain loudly about a loss of the human. We recognize that individual sociotechnologies vary in benefits; most individual systems are neither completely good nor completely bad. Attention to individual systems surely is important, for example, health care or campaign finance systems. Yet a piecemeal upgrading has negligible likelihood of reforming a critical mass of systems within an effective time frame.

What Will It Be Like If Machine Systems Rule the World?

Machine systems, as tools, have now evolved to a third conceptual level. The first level is when a machine system is a tool in the Aristotelian sense. This is when a tool is an extension of a person, increasing his capability, for example, as in a knife that allows him better to cut butter. A second level, well recognized, is when the tool becomes an important shaper of the tool user. To an extent, this was the case with the knife, which also helped shape the lives of soldiers and others. But there is a more significant shaping at the second level. The car is a tool that allows people better to travel. At the same time, it shapes whole populations of lives and habitats. People working within the automobile industry are shaped by the technology of the car, and people using cars lead changed lives. Even the lives of those without cars are transformed as their cities change. The suburbs are encouraged, and we have the donut design of many modern American cities. The third level is when interconnected and higher-speed machine systems lurch as if toward independence from the humans using them. Again, this was the case to some extent at the previous level, as nowadays few people feel able to live without cars. But there is a quantum change. Missile defense systems provide an example, if we recall how close machine systems came to annihilating the world during the Cuban Missile Crisis and in the mid-1990s.

There is the prospect of a fourth level characterized by machine system domination. Froglets can symbolize such a level, even if they never exist. Moravec (1998) describes froglets as having the size of a computer chip and as having little arms that can lock onto other froglets' arms. He tells us that our coming world will be dominated by froglets, because houses and all kinds of buildings can be self-made by, and out of, froglets. Buildings can be "programmed" to construct themselves. The upside is that froglets, apparently, can be programmed to reproduce. The downside, we are told, is that the little inanimates could get out of control and consume all the raw and other materials in the world. Moravec predicts the end of human domination.

This talk of levels is misleading if it is not recognized that machine systems affect different individuals differently. The existence of a dialysis system does not have the same effect on a healthy individual as on an afflicted person, for instance; the political machine affects individuals in the political class differently than excluded individuals. The whole person-in-herself in-her-difference is the individual that counts.

Somewhere between the third and fourth levels, there will be more giant machine systems without human operatives. Against this, I want to say that the presence of the human provides something special and distinctive—something sublime—that could not be provided by a nonhuman. What will it be like when daily we encounter giant machines without people?

1. Imagine that it's forty years from now. Imagine entities like a fully automated chain of grocery stores, a fully automated Internal Revenue Service (IRS), and a fully automated penitentiary system: no employees, yet providing services. Electronically interconnected with whatever data systems they need (for information, feedback, and control), imagine that it's possible for these entities to provide all the services that are required (although it would do them differently). The difference is that there are no employees. What difference could the absence of the human element make? Is there anything special and distinctive that could be provided by the human as opposed to the nonhuman?

2. Imagine that it's sixty years from now. Imagine a fully automated hospital: no employees, yet providing efficient services. What difference could the absence of the human element make? Is there anything special and distinctive that could be provided by the human, as opposed to the nonhuman? Remember the reference in Essay 2 to the beneficial effects of skin-to-skin (kangaroo) care as opposed to incubator storage, for preterm infants (Feldman et al., 2002). It is also said that there are beneficial effects for babies in soothing music (Kaminski, 1996) and in standard rest periods (Torres et al., 1997).

3. Imagine that it's eighty years from now. Again, imagine that there is in institutions something special and distinctive that is provided by the human element or human, rather than nonhuman, machinery. Does this human element (if it exists) have a starring role or just a bit part? Should managers and thinkers continue to devote their main energies to making the humans work the nonhuman machinery better? Or should they spend more attention to making the nonhuman machinery work so that it helps the humans provide whatever special and distinctive output the humans provide? I think that humans should have a starring role, focusing on what is distinctively human.

The symbol of the machine system already rules governance, however. Many celebrate economic and political and bureaucratic governance in machine system and mere technicist terms, pinning their hopes on better systems. It makes sense to them. The symbol of the machine, the system, lives in our unconscious as we seek to understand governance. It can be repressed as people choose other models; but it lurks. The economy is seen as a gigantic and loose system or web of huge subsystems, for example, a gigantic system that some think operates best when it is left alone (see Essay 15). The term ":political machine" is often seen in negative terms, but a good machine secures reelections. Private and public bureaucracies are also seen in machine or technicist terms. The employees of a company as a machine exist for the machine. Functionaries function as tenders of the machine, especially the managers. The practice reinforces the symbolism, and the symbolism reinforces the practice.

As they become larger and become more integrated and intelligent, the machine systems surely become more independent. As globalization continues and intensifies, for instance, the economic system grows ever more independent of individual humans.

The best response is finesse, rather than force. I remember being encouraged in high school to look down my nose at Luddites, for the wrong reason. The scoffing was on the grounds that it is mindless to oppose "progress." Because progress is not simply whatever-changes-happen, I think that the high school basis for scoffing was itself mindless. If Gen. Ned Ludd were alive today, I hope that he would opt for finesse. Named after Gen. Ludd, the Luddites were active from 1812 to 1817 in destroying new power looms and other machines being introduced into factories. The machine-breaking spread through England's Midlands, site of the Industrial Revolution. Imposition of the death sentence (a law passed against Lord Byron's opposition) and the arrival of twelve thousand troops were enough to reestablish the common sense of progress as whatever-changes-happen.

To the extent that governance lurches into the third conceptual level of the machine system, it is unrealistic to take the line of Voltaire's Dr. Pangloss, echoing Leibniz and celebrating the claim that we live "in the best of all possible worlds." I agree with Max Weber, quoted in Essay 3, that such domination does not gel with our full and beautiful humanity. To the extent that machine systems develop, the Leviathan-like features will become felt more sharply. The words of Hermann Rauschning (1941) can be borrowed and adapted. "Leviathan is the universal world machine of which mankind are the operatives, and in which the only characterization is 'satisfactory or faulty material,' where human beings are as interchangeable as the spark plugs of a motor." Shudder at the prospect of a fourth conceptual level, a new medieval superstate where the machines are feudal lords!

What Should Practitioners Do About Machine Systems?

Practitioners should address machine system concerns through playing as thinking, justice-as-seeking, and practice as art. Changing the nature of systems is an option that I want to suggest. Unavailable is a thoroughly adequate programmatic formula for the *short-term* termination of this face of the king. I think it will take much longer—and much finesse from the practitioner's art.

Thinking as Playing

Developing the symbolic structure for a distinction between arrangement and system is a *gadfly* example, given here, of thinking as playing. The intent is that, as the word is resymbolized, *arrangements* should be recognized as concinnities that are more authentically hesitant (see Essay 10) and thus more human-friendly. To make it clear that I am not talking about arrangement in present terms, I will designate the new sense by "arrangement(s)" in quotes. I think of the Golden Rule as an example of a justice "arrangement," as suggested in Essay 11. Specifying operationally meaningful differences between "arrangement" and system might be sought in such terms as standing against (under thinking as playing), deconstructive attitude (under justice as seeking), and hesitation (under practice as art).

Symbolic resources for addressing machine system concerns have not been adequately developed, and they should be. Symbolic kits for distinguishing "arrangement" and for "standing against" are not yet available. On "arrangement," dictionary and other definitions describe arrangements as negligibly different from systems. A concinnity is a little better when it is described as a harmonious fitting together. But "arrangement" means more than this. The symbolic kit presently available does not help in reserving the concept of "arrangement" for a system that is *enough* of a nonsystem. Note the word *enough!* The present kit of symbols makes it hard to specify a harmonious fitting together that is *enough* of a harmonious nonfitting-together, facilitating an "arrangement" that relates appropriately to the whole person-in-herself in-her-difference. The resymbolization, with a word like "arrangement" or a snappier label, is what is central.

Practitioners should play with insights like *standing against,* applying the notion differently to "arrangements" and systems. *Standing against* can be approached by considering Marcuse's account of the flattening out of the antagonism between culture and social reality in the rationalizing context that accompanies capitalism (Marcuse, 1991, 56ff). He claims (1991, 57) that this flattening out has obliterated the "oppositional, alien, and transcendental elements in the higher culture by virtue of which it constituted another dimension of reality." Associating with this, I have gone on to think of the losing battle of musicians like Anton Weber, wanting to liberate music from the hierarchical structures placed on it by tonality. Weber's music *stands against* the existing musical system in seeing each individual tone as having its own expressive possibilities, independent of the traditional discourse of harmony. With adequate resymbolization, practitioners inclined to stand against their own systems could contribute to transforming those systems into "arrangements."

Justice as Seeking

The possibility of transforming systems into de facto "arrangements" through a deconstructive attitude is the example of justice-as-seeking offered here. This can facilitate the symbolic distinction between systems and "arrangements." By deconstructive attitude,

I am referring to Jacques Derrida's claim that "deconstruction is justice" and to Drucilla Cornell's corollary about infinite responsibility (Cornell et al., 1992).

Deconstruction is described as justice because it is a good reading of a text, where text refers to any account of any event or activity or life. Because of the nature of language, texts (any accounts of any event or activity or life) are replete with metaphors and binary oppositions. Look at this, or any other, book; it is impossible to write, or read, without metaphors. Look at Ambrogio Lorenzetti's *Allegory of Good Government and Allegory of Bad Government* frescoes, painted 160 years before Michelangelo, down the road from Florence in Siena. Metaphor and binary oppositions are what the paintings are about. Yet the most invidious metaphors are the many that are not at all obvious, and a favorite example (mentioned in Essay 1) is that Newtonian physics is infused with the metaphor of a mechanical universe. Binary oppositions are statements like good and bad, economic and political, and (mark this) post-traditional governance and traditional governance. These metaphors and binary oppositions exist in a jumbled way in any text. Deconstruction can uncover the metaphors and show how they affect the meaning. The oppositions can be deconstructed, revealing in-between traces. There is meaning in the text at whatever level of deconstruction is chosen; but the text can always be deconstructed further and yet further. The upshot is that the text is, ultimately and finally, *undecidable*. Thus, reading the text of governance in this way has been described as a matter of justice.

Drucilla Cornell (1992) writes of infinite responsibility for bloodless bureaucratic violence that results from undecidability, and this responsibility applies to men of systems (see Adam Smith's use of this term at the head of this third section of the book). The official with a deconstructive attitude cannot say that her actions are determined by a normative imperative (a justice reason) for her to follow the system. The administrator cannot say that justice requires her to do X; the judge cannot say that justice requires her to pass this or that sentence; and so on. Cornell argues that undecidability imposes infinite responsibility on us. For her, it is false that undecidability alleviates responsibility. She means that practitioners who enforce (or enact) laws must recognize that they cannot justify their actions by appealing to legal or other systems or to a superior's orders.

Viewed in this way, the governing system may be nudged toward a de facto "arrangement." One of the members of the Texas Parole Board, which reviews execution appeals from the many criminals who are executed in that state, is reported in *George* (September 2000) as saying, "I do not have the right to make my own moral judgments. I have an obligation to follow what the system prescribes." No, Mr. Parole Board Member, Cornell would say—and I say—that you should take unlimited responsibility on your own personal shoulders for each and every aspect of your official acts. The man of system bears infinite responsibility, and he is accountable without limit. Officials like the Texas Parole Board member cannot take refuge in appeals to the moral imperative, the justice, of the system. To the extent that the man of system recognizes this, the suggestion is that systems can be transformed toward "arrangements."

Practice as Art

Managing day-to-day systems with authentic hesitation, it is suggested, can also contribute toward transforming systems into "arrangements." The example offered here, authentic hesitation, is close cousin to the deconstructive attitude.

A governance framework should include "arrangements"—and some systems—for activities like picking up garbage, protecting runaway children, preserving parks and forests, and all the other under-the-nails practicalia that facilitates a better quality of life. Yet the suggestion is that we are oversystematized. Systems are created and managed by men of systems who typically lack the authentic hesitation they should have—lacking a preference for authentic hesitation in the style of holding and expressing our own and our group's prescriptions. Such a lack is exemplified by another Texas Parole Board member who said that, in denying execution appeals, he was encouraged by his belief that he was sending executed people to a better place.

It is understood that public and private governments will continue to conduct politics and to make policies, to pass legislation
directed at particular problem categories and to administer. Practice as art can work in, as it were, the interstices, embracing the
day-to-day with the larger question of the interrelationship of
the totality of systems and the individual human. The suggestion
is that, as part of this, it could encourage managers—the men of
systems—to foster authentic hesitation in creating and administering governance "arrangements." The aim could be, at the very
minimum, to tweak practice.

Authentic hesitation can take various forms. For instance, practice as art could secure hesitation by setting systems against systems. Some computer systems have been helpful in loosening or
eliminating some other administrative systems, as governance is
able to administer without relying so much upon rigid rules. Such
computer systems may allow governance to deal more directly
with the individual. Computerization that permits fixed assembly
line systems to become more tailored is suggestive of the kind of
change that could be sought. The existence of audit or inspector
general systems examining operating systems is suggestive of setting systems against systems. Yet, this has the disadvantage of creating yet another set of systems.

In setting systems against systems, it would be helpful to set
symbolic systems (that too is *now* called systems) against governance systems. With appropriate resymbolization, more will become possible. For instance, there is a value in resymbolizing
totalizing and *individualizing*. Foucault contrasts the two, applying and distinguishing between the symbols of city game and shepherd game. Totalizing leads to rule-making, what happens in
governing a population or a subgroup. Individualizing can extend
to what it is to govern a particular whole person-in-herself in-her-
difference. We must return to this in Essay 18. For Foucault, the
city game refers to creating laws and policy rules and regulations
(systems) that concern populations and subgroups of populations.
The shepherd game, concerning pastoral power, is directed at the
care of each individual sheep in her or his differences. With
resymbolization, the concept of a shepherd game can become

elevated to the commonsense status now enjoyed by totalizing. Practice as art, including thinking as playing, can encourage a war between fresh symbolic systems and unwanted bureaucratic systems.

What I Expect

Think of a radically different symbolization of governance! Kill the king, who manifests himself in a variety of faces! I repeat that Essay 14 writes about power-over, the majesty of the king in traditional government and especially in the public bureaucracy. Essay 15 is about the unexamined rhetoric of power-over, especially in the private sector. Essay 16 speaks of cruelty as a face of the king, being cruel to be kind. Essay 17 talks about the coldness of mere efficiency, not love, as the face of the king; Essay 18 points to the many-faced king as the figure of hierarchical democracy, as the political boss. Overall, what is wrong is the traditional way of looking at governance. The regicide is directed at the traditional symbolic language.

I expect a better world from a killing of the king. Michelangelo's David statue too is about killing the enemy—eyes "watchful . . . the neck of a bull . . . hands of a killer . . . the body a reservoir of energy" (Bonner, 2004). The traditional way of looking at governance should be transcended. Terminated would be highly undesirable features, all socially constructed, like those described in these essays on practice as art. From that killing I expect a better quality of life for each individual whole human-in-herself in-her-difference. I expect the hand of bureaucracy to become lighter, especially as practitioner attention is broadened from immediate short-run concerns to include longer-run understandings like those discussed in this essay between totality and individuality. As a bureaucrat, I want to be more than a cog in the machine.

14 • Visible Hand: Cult of the Leader

Practice as art should seek the longer-run termination of the cult of the leader. As long as it values leadership, governance should embrace the art of just, rather than heroic, leadership. The cult of the leader is systemic. It is a systemic feature of the symbolic repertoire of what counts as the civilizing process in society. The examples focus mainly on the visible hand of leadership in traditional government, especially in public bureaucracy; but the conclusions apply throughout governance.

> While the great lord passes the wise peasant
> bows deeply and silently farts.
>
> —*Ethiopian proverb, reported in Scott, 1990*

Machiavelli urges that the effective leader must be prepared to go to Hell. His prince should be willing to do whatever is ethically good and equally willing to do whatever is ethically bad; the prince must do whatever it takes. Politics for him is detached from morality; one might say that politics has its own morality. Machiavelli insists that the world of politics is different from the world of good people.

On the contrary, the leader should refuse to go to Hell. Instead, she should seek to eliminate in the longer run the very cult of the leader. Or, to put it another way, practice as art should include the longer-run aim of terminating societal dependence on the cult of leadership. As something over and above ordinary management, leadership is a fetish. On one meaning describing societies called "primitive," *fetish* refers to an object believed to have magical powers. Societies relying on leadership are in that respect primitive.

The first section of this essay speaks of the proposed refusal of the cult. It also suggests that, as long as it values leadership, governance practice should transcend heroic leadership. The second section concerns the systemic character of the urge for leadership, giving the example of deference to leadership in public bureaucracy. In the third section I describe the urge for leadership as a function of the symbolic repertoire of what counts as civilizing.

Leadership No!

Abandon the cult of leader! I've mentioned that practice as art should focus on the long-run eradication of the societal fetish of leader. Here I'm going to note another root, the individual psychological. In the interim, abandon adoration of the heroic leader! The practitioner's art should refuse the role of heroic leader and embrace—self-leadership, if you like—the just model described in Essays 7 through 12.

The Fetish of Leader

In the psychopathology of fetishism, the sexual focus is on objects that are intimately associated with the human body, like shoes and pantyhose. In leader as fetish, the focus is on an object associated with the body politic.

Kaplan et al. (2003, 720) explain that "the particular fetish is linked to someone closely involved with the patient during childhood and has a quality associated with this loved, needed, or even traumatizing person." They explain that the psychological disorder begins in adolescence, but the fetish might be established in early childhood. I read that Freud describes the fetish as a symbol of the phallus for males (fetishism is mainly a male psychopathology) with castration fears. The *Diagnostic and Statistical Manual of Mental Disorders* (American Psychiatric Association, 2000) provides that the "fantasies, sexual urges, or behaviors cause clinically significant distress or impairment in social occupational or other important areas of functioning." In leader as fetish, I imagine that the "loved, needed, or even traumatizing person" is a daddy or mommy figure, like a biological parent or a schoolteacher or a local bully.

The Short Run

Abandon heroic leadership! Cesare Borgia is Machiavelli's ideal prince. Machiavelli describes with approval how Borgia *cleverly* tricked the Orsini leaders into trusting and how Borgia then strangled them. A better model for just leadership is not Cesare Borgia but someone like Martin Luther King. As long as we want leaders, practice as art should surely seek the company of the just, the companionship of good people.

Machiavelli in *The Prince* proposes a new statesmanship and a new politics guided by considerations of expediency. His world of politics is dominated by swindle and risk, and people are by nature ungrateful, fickle, deceitful, cowardly, restless, greedy. The prince must caress and hurt, forgive and punish, benefit and suppress. Famously, Machiavelli believed that the prince should aim to be loved and to be feared; but, if he must choose, he should choose to be feared. It is in such circumstances that Machiavelli held that the leader must not be bound within ethical limits appropriate for private citizens. Princely virtue, for him, is single-minded eagerness to dominate, to exercise power-over.

Can a contrast be drawn between the just leadership of, say, Aung San Suu Kyi and the heroic leadership of, say, Napoleon Bonaparte?—parallel to the just leadership of Martin Luther King and the heroic leadership of Machiavelli's prince? Kyi is general secretary of the National League for Democracy in Burma, and she won the 1991 Nobel Prize for Peace for her "nonviolent struggle for democracy and human rights." She became in 1988 the leader of Burma's democratic opposition. She and her party won the Burmese election in 1990. But the military regime ignored the election results and has since kept her under house arrest. As the Nobel Committee chair said, Aung San Suu Kyi "unites a deep commitment and tenacity with a vision in which the ends and means form a single unit. Its most important elements are democracy, respect for human rights, reconciliation between groups, non-violence and personal and collective discipline" (Adams, 1993). Napoleon Bonaparte is well known as, after being first consul, the emperor of France from 1804 to 1815.

Perhaps! On the one hand, Kyi and Bonaparte can be distinguished in terms, for instance, of violence, autocracy, ethics, and style. Kyi is dedicated to nonviolence; Bonaparte was one of history's greatest warriors. Kyi exhibits humility; Bonaparte crowned himself, while even the pope is made to sit by. For Kyi's leading ethic, see the quote above from the Nobel Committee chair. For Bonaparte, a leading ethic is loyalty to Bonaparte; he was an emperor who set up relatives as kings. The style of Napoleon Bonaparte is not only the great reformer but also the leader high on a white horse, the general whose mere presence translates into additional military power. That is not Aung San Suu Kyi's style.

This comparison between Kyi (as just leader) and Napoleon (as heroic leader) is misleading on the other hand. Leadership that is heroic need not embrace Machiavelli's principle. King Frederick the Great, an essayist attempting to refute Machiavelli's ideas, would want to point that out. Also, different types of leadership are consistent with Machiavelli's principle of a new politics guided by expediency. Then again, some onlookers may be attracted to Kyi precisely because she evokes a romantic reaction to her heroism —a romantic reaction fired by her great strength and dignity in adversity. An American (or Frenchman) has no less a romantic attitude when he "believes in" the majesty of his nation's presidency and when his heart jumps on hearing "Hail to the Chief" (or "La Marseillaise"). *"Allons enfants de la Patrie. La jour de gloire est arrivé . . ."* It is easy to deceive ourselves on matters like leadership, where the symbolic structures of psychology and society are so powerful. It is not unimportant that Carl Jung identified the leader as an archetype that inhabits our collective unconscious.

The contrast between just and heroic leadership is intended to add to the suggestion that the post-traditional practitioner, public and private, should oppose an ethic of power-down. Recall that practice as art should embrace elimination of society's dependence on the idea of leader. Recall another point already mentioned: as long as society demands leaders, the post-traditional practitioner should adopt the model of just leadership described in Essays 7 through 12. The post-traditional practitioner should engage her day-to-day activities with consciousness of opposition to an ethic of power-down. The "crime" of the cult of the leader was well recognized, oddly, in the old Soviet Union, which practiced tyranny. The violence of the cult of the leader is ill understood, equally oddly, in many democratic countries that pride themselves on the practice of democracy. The cult is so ingrained psychologically and socially that most cannot imagine a society without hierarchy.

Cult of Leadership in Public Bureaucracy

> With rare, but significant, exceptions the public performance of the subordinate will, out of prudence, fear and the desire to curry favor, be shaped to appeal to the expectations of the powerful.
>
> —*Scott*

There is a systemic character in the urge for the cult of leadership, and it extends throughout governance. It is crystallized in the deference to leadership in public bureaucracy and in thinking about bureaucracy, and this is the illustration offered in this section. The leader principle pervades bureaucratic thinking, just as it pervades economic theory and practice, politics, and personal lives.

Practice as art should refuse the one-dimensionality of the thinking that regards the leadership cult as mere common sense. Relevent is Herbert Marcuse's description (1991)—described in a moment—of a great refusal of the one-dimensionality in thinking that uncritically accepts existing structures and norms.

The Case of Public Bureaucracy

> Domination is transfigured into administration.
>
> —*Marcuse*

There is a steep *net* top-down tilt in public bureaucratic thinking and practice, despite the exceptions. The tilt is manifested in behavior, like the choice of questions and prescriptions. Speaking-from-power and acting-from-power are standard in traditional administrative thinking in such respects as (first) the emphasis on values like leadership, in (second) the hierarchical role of the very idea of administration, in (third) day-to-day personnel relationships, and in (fourth) the way that bureaucratic topics are discussed.

Economic practice and theory are no less hierarchical than public administration thinking and practice. Essay 15 describes the top-down structure of corporations and notes the centrality in economic theory of the entrepreneur.

First in the case of public bureaucracy, leadership as a value and as an activity features prominently in traditional public administration thinking. If there were no top-down tilt, for instance, the choice of questions and perspectives would include less about seeking and nurturing leaders—executive managers rather than mere managers. Second, the very idea of administration has a hierarchical relationship to programs in most traditional thinking. Traditionally, to administer is to direct program activities; administrators administer subordinate program specialists, and that is one reason they are usually paid higher salaries.

Third, Scott is right to point out (1990, 28) that on "a daily basis, the impact of power is more readily observed in acts of deference, subordination and ingratiation." Yet subordination, ingratiation, and deference are not adequately represented in theorizing the modern manager, the modern leader. Managers not only do old-fashioned POSDCORB functions (planning, organizing, staffing, directing, coordinating, reporting, budgeting); they also SID (subordinate, ingratiate, defer), at least to their superiors. Fourth, hierarchy is assumed in the way that administrative functions— like budgeting, reporting, and staffing—are traditionally discussed. Don't budgeteers rightly assume a process of approval up the chain? The steepness of the hierarchy is exemplified in the language of the typical job description. As mentioned before, directing, coordinating, and controlling *all* the personnel and activities of the assigned unit is a job description worthy of a king.

Do you remember the first, or the last, time that you openly confronted *the* boss with your hidden transcript that challenged the foundation of *her* public transcript? Scott (1990) distinguishes between two types of transcript, where a transcript refers to a person or group in terms of both their speech acts and nonspeech acts, like gestures. Public transcripts for him are what is "openly avowed to the other party in a power relationship" (Scott, 1990, 2). Hidden transcripts contain what is concealed. The "public transcript is—barring a crisis —systematically skewed in the direction of the libretto, the discourse, represented by the dominant" (Scott, 1990, 4). The public transcript is "the self-portrait of the dominant elite as they would have themselves seen" (Scott, 1990, 18)—designed to impress.

Isn't (say) mainstream public administration theory and thinking a *mere* public transcript? I think so. Shouldn't the content of traditional public administration theory be seen as what subordinates dare say openly to superiors? I believe so. For instance, those hell-bent to appear "practical" to their powers-that-be may be discouraged to highlight the issue(s) of surveillance that is described as a growing feature of modernity. For surveillance, see Dandeker, 1990, a book that explores "the relationships between bureaucracy and surveillance in modern capitalism." Parallel to economic theory, I suggest that public administration theory as-a-whole is an apology for administrative practice. It is an apology in the sense that traditional theory wants to engineer and reengineer—to fix— any administrative imperfections. It is an apology in the sense that the laity is assured that bureaucracy does not have any unfixable machinery.

Not all administrative and organization theory and practice reflects a speaking-from-power perspective, however. Nowadays, matrix organizations are widely used and discussed; toward the "beginning," Frederick Taylor wrote about functional management. Mary Parker Follett repeated the well-known distinction between "power" and "power-over." In practice, we all know of relatively egalitarian small groups, for example, in management analysis or computer groups—bands of brothers and sisters.

Refusal

Marcuse's account (1991) of a great refusal is relevant to a refusal of the cult of leadership. It is unlikely, for one thing, that a refusal of the leadership cult can take place without consideration of the wider cultural picture that Marcuse describes. His great refusal is a refusal of all forms of oppression and domination. It is opposed to what he calls "the new conformism which is a facet of technological rationality translated into social behavior" (Marcuse, 1991, 84).

Such a great refusal, without being limited to the sole topic of leadership, has been discussed by post-traditional thinkers. For example, there are the six papers in a June 2003 symposium.

In that symposium, O.C. McSwite (2003, 183–204) discusses the great refusal in terms of a turn for public administration toward the worlds of discourse and symbols. McSwite describes the success of the turn as depending "on those who have the insight and the inclination to let go of illusions of the societal order, assume a position as 'masterless people,' and be in a process of active collaboration through the venue of their distinctive singularities." Patricia M. Patterson (2003, 233–242) in the same symposium writes of the great refusal in terms of Yeats's poem that includes the line "The best lack all conviction, while the worst / Are full of passionate intensity." Richard Box (2003, 243–260) analyzes Marcuse's claim of a contradiction between, on the one hand, a life of material plenty buttressed by instrumental thought and, on the other hand, a life that a human might prefer if she were free from the chains of power relations.

Lisa Zanetti (2003, 261–276) urges public administrators to learn to think differently. She suggests that they should "learn and practice the art of holding contradictions: that is, by refusing to rush to resolution of contradiction in the policy implementation process." Louis Howe (2003, 277–298) analyzes refusal in terms of subaltern ethics. He ends his paper by reporting what Foucault once suggested. "Maybe the target nowadays is not to discover what we are, but to refuse what we are." It was in that same symposium that I (2003, 205–232) wrote about three levels of reality relevant to a great refusal of speaking-from-power.

Symbolic Character of the Leadership Cult

> Without a master, one cannot be cleaned.
>
> —*Dominique Laporte*

The cult is systemic, and it is nourished by society's symbolic systems. Abandoning a cult of leadership requires recognizing roots in the symbolic that pervades society. The celebration of power-over has symbolic roots crystallized in governance and bureaucracy and in the societal view of what is civilized.

I distinguish three layers of a cult of leadership. These layers are (a) the transparent, (b) the disciplinary symbolic, and (c) the cloacal symbolic. The transparent layer refers to the *nonsymbolic elements in both governance and bureaucracy.*

The disciplinary symbolic layer refers to *symbols and symbolizations that, first, are relevant to choice of a speaking-from-power or a speaking-to-power perspective and, second, are within a particular discipline or field.* Examples of disciplines or fields are economics, political science, public administration, and business administration.

The third or cloacal symbolic layer refers to *societal symbolizations that, first, are relevant to what-is-counted-as-civilized and, second, are not specifically in disciplines or fields*—unlike those at the disciplinary symbolic level. It is especially related to the action of the sewer, to what is counted as excrement. "Cloacae: sewers" explains James Joyce (1997, 181), and "cloacal" is the adjective.

The three layers are equally real, albeit not equally important. I have explained that I'm sensitive to philosophical difficulties in discussing the real (e.g., see Farmer, 1990, 29–34). Let's avoid these conversations by saying that all three layers are equally real, insofar as any one layer is real. In the same manner, let's agree that there is a range of layers, and that others may want to identify a different number of them.

The theory is that, at the cloacal symbolic layer and acting on both the transparent and the disciplinary symbolic, the top-down character of governance is absorbed from the "civilizing" action of society.

Disciplinary Symbolic Level

The disciplinary symbolic layer shapes, just as it reflects, what is included and what is excluded at the transparent and cloacal levels. In discussing this level, I'm continuing with the example of public bureaucracy. So, please consider the self-definition of the field of public administration. The poverty of the self-definition crimps public administration's proclivity to speak to power.

Recall two traditional public administration self-definitions. The first, popular (not now) during PA's infancy and therefore during its formative stage, speaks of "getting things done through people." The second self-definition speaks about "executing the will of legitimate political and other authorities."

Such definitions set symbolic limits on what is legitimate public administration talk. First, the "getting things done through people" version privileges public administration talk about "things." Symbolically illegitimate is talk about the symbolic.

Second, for the "executing the will of legitimate political and other authorities" version, traditional public administration is a subject that expresses itself as dedicated to achieving whatever legitimate powers-that-be want done. In a sense, public administration's raison d'etre is to facilitate speaking-from-power and acting-from-power. Public administration, on this self-definition, is a tool for legitimate societal power. This goes some way toward explaining traditional public administration's reluctance at the transparent level to look at a larger or macro picture. Thoughts about micro concerns are privileged because they do not involve fundamental changes in the existing structure of society.

Traditional public-administration-theory-as-a-whole is largely a celebration of the status quo, sustaining and privileging the midlevel practitioner. It celebrates through subservience to here-and-now practitioners, especially to the midlevel practitioners. Fee-paying student fodder for the education mill! Look at the curricula of public administration educational programs. Look at the literature. Public administration here-and-now practice is so dominant over traditional theorizing, for instance, that the dominance typically seems necessary. Many traditional public administration theorists tend to act as if they *need* justification from the here-and-now practitioners. The result of this dominator-submissive relationship of practice to theory in traditional public administration is not trivial. Rather, it is a factor in waving off traditional public-administration-theory-as-a-whole from speaking-to-power issues.

There is a curious difference of target levels between the celebration in the cases of public administration and of (see Essay 15) economics. While the rhetoric of traditional public administration is firmly grounded on the midlevel practitioner-we-have, the hero of microeconomic theory is the high-level entrepreneur. Mainstream economic-theory-as-a-whole, by comparison, does not kowtow to the local chamber of commerce; and, as Herbert Simon noticed, microeconomic theory focuses on "the firm" rather than on particular "real-life" firms. Antiestablishment issues do exist in the heart of economic theory; the critique of monopolies is an example. Such "antipower" perspectives are discouraged by the self-definition of traditional public administration.

Cloacal Symbolic Level

> Language speaks and asks: why am I beautiful?
> Because my master bathes me.
>
> —Paul Eluard

Laporte (1993) suggests in her scholarly book *History of Shit* that there is a connection between a hierarchy of power and "civilizing" fecal cleanliness; and between the "civilizing" action of a hierarchy of power and what-counts-as-truth (in, say, public administration). But the civilizing bathing is not just a cleaning of physical fecal matter. Also it is a cleaning of what-counts-as-true, what-counts-as-true-in-language. Laporte begins with two royal events that occurred in 1539. In that year, on "the day of the Immaculate Virgin impregnated by the Word," King Francois took a step in the cleaning of the French language. His bathing edict was that henceforth all courts would issue edicts in "no other than the maternal French." The Latin excrement would be eliminated. Later that year he imposed sweeping requirements on citizens concerning the disposal of *merde* (it's difficult to write the word in plain English for a book, as opposed to a wall) and other remnants of earth. But Laporte goes further in her claim that one *requires* a master in order to be "cleaned." Of language as the conveyor of what-counts-as-true, Laporte (1993, 7) observes that "If language is beautiful, it must be because a master bathes it—a master who cleans shit holes, sweeps offal, and expurgates city and speech to confer upon them order and beauty."

It is in the light of this that we turn to Freud's claim (1961, ch. 2 & 3) that cleanliness, order, and beauty are requirements of civilization. Freud is not quite right. It is about *what-counts-as*. He should have said that civilization's requirements are what-counts-as-cleanliness, what-counts-as-order, and what-counts-as-beauty. What-counts-as-civilized serves to enforce a top-down perspective. Bear in mind that what is suppressed by speaking-from-power can often be—in another version of what-counts-as-civilization—sublimely beautiful, orderly, and clean. Read Paul Eluard's 1926 lines, quoted at the head of this subsection. The impact of the cloacal symbolic process is to nourish the top-down.

The cloacal sense of what counts as cleanliness, order, and beauty is reflected in the clean, orderly, and beautiful analyses in economics. Charts drawn about the economics of the firm, for instance, have all these qualities. There is the mathematical cleanliness, order, and beauty of economic analysis, even when speaking of the most grubby of material matters. The cloacal sense of cleanliness, order, and beauty is also reflected in public administration. Rejected from theorizing about the field are uncomfortable features that are inconsistent with the kind of *public administration facts* that McSwite (1998) describes as part of the life of any organization—what counts as dirty, inappropriate, and uncivilized.

Traditional governance thinking is within the cloacal constraints of what-counts-as-reason, what-counts-as-true, what-counts-as-appropriate. These socially constructed constraints serve as dominant signifiers for governance. Traditional thinking and practice are shaped by a modernist emphasis on what-counts-as-reason, for example. Features given less emphasis from what-counts-as-reason include the unreasoning (see Essay 6) of which Michel Foucault and others speak. What-counts-as-reason, what-counts-as-true, and what-counts-as-appropriate have emerged from a bathing by the powers-that-be. In the sense of Eluard's lines (quoted above), they have emerged *beautiful*.

The cloacal function includes governance—like public administration and economics—carrying out what is counted as civilized, what is socially constructed as "civilization." What is counted as civilized is the leader, the cult of the leader.

Epilogue

Governmental buildings in Washington, D.C., solid and immense, symbolize the value of top-down governance systems and leadership. The ponderous messages engraved high on their sides are Moses-like, *speaking-from-power* symbols that seem to demand reverence. Office buildings in Manhattan and in Shanghai stand spectacular and scrape the sky. The Empire State and the Chrysler Buildings present a vision of the power and brilliance of our economic systems. They witness to our age of seduction, *speaking-from-power* that is wedded to wealth and the leadership mystique of the entrepreneur. The character of the Washington and New York buildings is a speaking-from-power-commercial. It invites us to look upward.

15 • Invisible Hand: Unexamined Rhetoric

Practice as art should engage the rhetoric of economics. Attention is drawn to the symbolic functioning of the invisible hand and of economic theory as a whole. It is also directed to economic corporations. This essay focuses on nontraditional government.

> The [New] Rhetoric must lead us through the Scramble, the Wrangle of the Market Place, the flurries and flare ups of the Human Barnyard, the Give and Take, the wavering line of pressure and counterpressure, the Logomachy, the onus of ownership, the Wars of Nerves.
>
> —*Kenneth Burke*

On the one hand, many applaud the invisible hand as optimal, for example, in supplying consumer demand. Over the past two hundred years, the structure of capitalist economies has been transformed; agriculture no longer accounts for 74 percent of American employment, for instance. Over the past one hundred years, ever newer goods and services have appeared. Look around at all the material goods and services we now have, including longer lives and better gadgets! Handy improvements!

On the other hand, others speak of such side effects as disempowerment, indignity, hunger, pain, inhumanity. Child sex slaves earn no money; if they try to escape, typically they are beaten or killed. The invisible hand supplies child slaves for kinky sex in response to consumer demand, efficiently. It is reported that a "sex-trafficking trade may begin in Eastern Europe and wend its way through Mexico, but it lands in the suburbs and cities of America" (Landesman, 2004, 32). Of one child-slave called Montserrat, the *New York Times Magazine* story reports that "Her cell of sex traffickers offered three ages of sex partners—toddlers to age four, five to twelve and teens—as well as what she called the damage group. In the damage group, (the slave-child) explained, 'Though sex always hurts when you are little, so it's always violent, everything was much more painful once you were placed in the damage group.'" (Landesman, 2004, 67). The harmful side effects are not confined to such infelicities as wooden two-by-fours that are not two by four inches, planned obsolescence, and quickie architecture.

Practice as art should engage the rhetoric of economics. In the first section of this essay, I speak about the rhetorical and apologetic function of Adam Smith's invisible hand. The second section points to misunderstandings about the economy and about the hand's side effects. The third section discusses the economic corporation. Kings still rule, economically speaking. The fourth section is about democratizing economic practice. The art of governance needs New Rhetoric to lead us through what Burke (1969, 42), quoted above, calls "the Scramble, the Wrangle of the Market Place, the flurries and flare ups of the Human Barnyard . . ."

The Rhetoric of the Invisible Hand

The rhetoric of the invisible hand is both an apology for and a celebration of the scramble and wrangle of capitalism. It can be both to the extent that an apology can be a celebration, and a celebration can be an apology. It is also an obscure symbol or metaphor, and this obscurity may account for some of its force— in the same way that St. Augustine thought that much of the rhetorical force of the Bible comes from its obscurity.

Like economic theory as a whole, the force of the invisible hand symbol makes it harder to think of alterations in the system of "free market capitalism"—a system-as-is that suits the interests of the power elite(s) and that was described in Essay 7 as at the center of our public ethics legacy. The invisible hand and economic theory as a whole symbolize economic forces as compatible ethically with naked self-interest and as independent of power-over. It is an independence-of-power-over that sits awkwardly beside critical features of economic practice such as the inequalities of wealth within and between nations.

Adam Smith's invisible hand, describing what he called the unfettered "propensity to truck, barter, exchange" (Campbell & Skinner, 1976, 26–27), can be interpreted in various ways. The traditional way is to understand the invisible hand doctrine as claiming that, when each person attempts to maximize her own individual satisfaction (to get all she can for herself, to gouge her neighbors), it is as if there were an "invisible hand" that arranges that society thereby achieves better outcomes than if each person had tried to act for the public interest. As Adam Smith put it, "It is not from the benevolence of the butcher, the brewer, or the baker, that we expect our dinner, but from their regard to their own interest. We address ourselves, not to their humanity but to their self-love, and never talk to them of our own necessities but of their advantages" (Campbell & Skinner, 1976, 26–27). It may be thought that it is perfectly ethical to kick and scratch my neighbors as I play in the scramble and wrangle of the marketplace, because everyone will be better off than if I actually try to help them. An alternative interpretation is to see the invisible hand as a metaphor for the automatic pricing mechanism that tends toward (if it does, in fact) a final equilibrium. Or, in a reverse direction, one can see the pricing system as a signature metaphor for the invisible hand.

The traditional interpretation of the invisible hand fits with a view well known to have been common in Adam Smith's eighteenth century, and this view was that some private vices are beneficial to society. Recall Bernard de Mandeville's *Fable of the Bees* (1714/1970). "That every Part was full of Vice, Yet the whole Mass a Paradise." His point is that private vices like luxury, greed, and envy all lead to public benefits by encouraging enterprise. The hive was doing famously while the bees were pursuing their own self-interest, bees smelling the flowers and sucking up the nectar. "While Luxury / Employ'd a Million of the Poor / And odious

Pride a Million more / Envy itself, and Vanity / Were Ministers of Industry." Yet, when the bees reformed (when the "knaves turn'd honest"), disaster struck the now-grumbling hive.

Adam Smith might not have had in mind as beneficent an invisible hand as we now suppose, as Rothschild (2001) points out. She argues persuasively that Smith's text does not attach as much weight to the invisible hand metaphor as do twentieth and twenty-first-century commentators. Beyond that, the interesting point she makes is that an eighteenth-century thinker would tend to "see" an invisible hand in more ominous symbolic terms than we do—as the hand behind the back that carries a dagger. Smith was a close student and admirer of Shakespeare and Voltaire, and—naturally enough as a Scot—he had an especially close interest in *Macbeth*. Just before the murder of Banquo, Macbeth (act 3, scene 2, 46–50) speaks of a bloody and invisible hand.

> . . . . Come, seeling night,
> Scarf up the tender eye of pitiful day;
> And with thy bloody and invisible hand
> Cancel and tear to pieces that great bond
> Which keeps me pale!

Smith was also an admirer of Voltaire's *Oedipe*. This is the play in which Oedipus is twice threatened by invisible hands.

Unsurprisingly, the story of the symbols within economic theory is more complicated than this, because in any discipline metaphor piles upon metaphor. It bears repeating that symbols interact, interweave. Symbolic action extends between symbols and parts of symbols, with complexity suggestive of organic chemistry. There are even symbols within symbols, for example, symbols within the symbol that is economics-as-a-whole. So the economics story houses other signature metaphors—supply and demand, the will for equilibrium, the searching at the margin, and equilibrium. Look with a lantern into any part of economics, any nook or cranny; there lurks the metaphor of supply and demand!

A familiar story—the hands-off account of economics—is that mainstream economic theory opposes economic engineering *tout court*. Many will insist on this to the point of apoplexy, and they are not wrong. Shapiro (1993, 103) points out that there are two poles in treating the social, emphasizing harmony and emphasizing disharmony. Smith's invisible hand, and the law of supply and demand that works toward equilibrium, is in the first category. Shapiro claims that Adam Smith's poetic language is on the side that assumes the existence of God as the universe's author, but an author who has left behind the mechanisms guaranteeing that the self and other are always congruent. He holds that the congruence is not a characteristic of the world but rather a metaphor, a trope, in the organization of Smith's economic thinking.

Equally reasonable is a hands-on reading of what is symbolized by economic-theory-as-a-whole. We can call the reading "deviant," but it is not outside the mainstream economic tradition. Economic-theory-as-a-whole is a symbol of celebration in that it "rejoices" that, properly engineered, general equilibrium is achieved. Economies tend to develop structural imperfections like monopolies (as noted in a moment, referring to Samuelson and Nordhaus), and the invisible hand needs a hand from the economic engineer. Even in Adam Smith's account, the invisible hand does not work optimally without "rivalrous competition." Economic-theory-as-a-whole is a symbol of apology to the extent that it "proves" how, properly engineered, market economic practice is optimal. Can do! The apology and the celebration is that economic-theory-as-a-whole is up to the task of providing whatever maintenance engineering is needed. Shapiro's "divine" interpretation may not have been quite right in its story of God reconciling self and other without human assistance. Instead, God may have provided man (it's always man!) with a fully effective do-it-yourself economic repair kit.

Recall that not all economic theorizing is mainstream, however. (For descriptions, see, for example, Arestis et al., 2001.)

There is arbitrariness about the shape of mainstream economic theory, and that is another reason why we should think about constitutive symbols like the invisible hand. Neoclassical economic theory is essentially deductive, for instance, and (as exemplified by Gustav von Schmoller, championing German historicism) it need not have been. Also, neoclassical economic theory stops short in offering explanations for the development of society. There is nothing like the grand sweep of the Marxian dynamic of societal development, where the substructure—interactive with the super-structure—functions like a kind of unconscious in propelling class and other arrangements. There is little like the stages of society that Adam Smith proposes.

Segregation and Lack

Nobel Prize winner Paul Samuelson, with Nordhaus, explains what he considers to be the invisible hand's failures. He does so in his mainstream textbook (Samuelson & Nordhaus, 1989). These side effects are inefficiency, inequality, and instability. Inefficiency occurs when the market contains monopolies, oligopolies, externalities, and public goods. Inequality refers to inequalities of income and wealth. Instability occurs in terms of inflation, unemployment, and low growth. As Samuelson and Nordhaus discuss, government can take corrective action. Inefficiency can be attacked through such measures, for example, as antitrust legislation. Instability can be counteracted through macroeconomic policies such as monetary and fiscal policies. Inequality can be combated (anathema for some!) by redistributing incomes through progressive taxation and income-support programs. The short-comings can be remedied—sometimes and to some extent.

When it comes to leading ourselves through the flurries and flare-ups of the Human Barnyard (see the quote above from Burke), the economy presents societal options that are broader than many want to recognize. We should not be limited by segregation be-tween *things economic* and *things noneconomic*. We need not be limited by lack in our rhetoric about capitalism.

Segregating the Economic

Samuelson and Nordhaus's account is true, but misleading. (I'm not saying that the authors do not realize it; it is that they are writing a text for students of economics.) Significantly, the rhetoric of the text treats the market as if it were something separate from a set of laws and separate from government. The rhetoric assumes the feasibility of an economic market that could stand alone without a network of criminal and civil laws, for example, bankruptcy or liability or criminal laws. No, there never has been a market as a kind of virgin forest, absent a set of laws. The rhetoric also assumes that it is false to claim that a dynamic part—some would say *the* most dynamic part—of the market is the creative public sector, where risky new developments result from governmental research. The Internet and the computer were public, not private, sector developments that were later turned over to the profit-making sector, for instance. Long has this been the pattern; an earlier example was the development in the naval context of a capability of firing from one moving platform to hit another moving platform. Equally misleading is speaking of *side effects,* as if the bad is separate from the "real thing." Samuelson and Nordhaus's text sidesteps the effect of capitalism on the social bond, for instance; recall that Frank Knight, the founding dean of the orthodox Chicago school of economics, pointed out that economic self-interest is insufficient as a bond that can keep society together. On the contrary, central to the productive energy of the raw self-interest of the invisible hand is a net weakening of the social bond(s).

Separation of the economic and noneconomic is artificial. It is an artifact primarily of the way that governance disciplines have developed. For example, it is both an economic and a noneconomic fact that the invisible hand privileges private, as compared with public, goods. By privileging private goods, I mean that the invisible hand shortchanges social infrastructure, public education, health care, and parks. Certainly, the separation between the economic and the noneconomic is often breached, for example, by political economy. Yet, when entering economic turf, thoughts are often regarded as second class if they are not in the style of the economics discipline. Noneconomists should feel even freer, leaving their disciplinary passports and their inhibitions at home.

Governance should include the economic sphere, I want to emphasize. As I have mentioned, it is through exploring the economic that most macro issues of public sector activity can be successfully addressed. (Conversely, it is through exploring the noneconomic that the largest and most critical issues of economic activity can be successfully addressed.) As an illustration of the importance of the economic, consider the stranglehold that corporate and other campaign contributions have on traditional government in the United States. It is no great secret that critical public policies —and perhaps some elections—are purchased. It is no secret that corruption is rampant in business transactions (e.g., Palast, 2003). As another illustration, consider the insights available from public choice economics. Public administration thinkers should say more about the charge of bloated public bureaucracies, for example. William Niskanen's model (Niskanen, 1971) of the budget-maximizing bureaucrat speaks of the workforce being twice the optimal size, for example, and I would like to know why a corresponding reduction is not possible. It is not enough to respond that government is basically good.

Practice as art should extend beyond the traditional scope of government. It should militate against an understanding of government confined to the merely political-administrative. Go to a private corporation, and see whether employees are governed/bossed and what percentage of employee waking time is spent at work. My preference is to understand nontraditional government only in terms of the larger corporations; choose any agreeable cutoff point. Others might want to go further and include other agencies involved in governance, such as nongovernmental organizations and other elements in civil society, for example, churches, unions, and even private schools. My hope is not to include corporations in more decision-making in government. Rather, it is to recognize that nontraditional government is a genuine part of governance.

Rhetorical Lack

Talk of the success or failure of *the* invisible hand is true, yet misleading, in another way. This misimpression is that capitalism is a unitary phenomenon, with unitary rhetoric. Options in reforming economies are broader than is often supposed. It is more than choosing between the invisible hand and no invisible hand. It is more than choosing between capitalism and varieties of socialism or bioregionalism. If capitalism is capitalism is capitalism and if the only alternative to capitalism is something like socialism, capitalism is privileged in many people's minds. That there are many varieties of capitalism is a truth that tends to be hidden, or repressed. The fact is that there is more than one form of capitalism even within the United States—and there could be many others, without being socialism or communism.

Different capitalisms can be created, even though we lump them all under the single heading *capitalism*. Samuelson and Nordhaus's account of the failures of the invisible hand can be used as a first illustration. There could be quantum varieties of inefficiency, inequality, and instability. If the differences really are quantum, distinct capitalisms would be created—even though we lump them under the same word. Road and rail could be used to offer a second illustration. A capitalist system that privileges private road transportation over public rail and other transportation is a different system from that where the reverse situation prevails. The differences are not at all trivial. For example, compare the effects of each system on city life. In neither the first nor the second illustration is there choice between free enterprise and un-free enterprise.

Economic Corporations

Krugman (2002) characterizes the present period in U.S. history as a new "gilded age" where the New Deal has been undone and where America is no longer "a middle class society." "As the rich get richer, they can buy a lot besides goods and services. Money buys political influence; it also buys intellectual influence" (Krugman, 2002, 76). (Kennickell, 2003, shows that wealth grew most strongly at the highest levels of the wealth distribution in the period from 1989 to 2001; the skewing has continued.) Politics has shifted more in favor of the wealthy.

Like economic society, the economic corporation is top-down. The "onus of ownership" (again borrowing Burke's words) is laden with *aristocratic* power. This is significant because of the importance of corporations in the world's economies. It will be recalled that about half of the world's one hundred biggest economies are corporations.

We have achieved political, but not economic, democracy. There is little democratic governance within the corporate gates, and the working of the invisible hand is deformed by the aristocratic form of the corporation. Look at the privileged position of stockholders, the disregard of employees and the community, and the human rights given to corporate persons.

There are large and relevant literatures on ideologies like anarchism, feminism, and ecologism. Each of the literatures is varied. Anarchism, for instance, includes the individualist, collectivist, communist, mutualist, and anarcho-syndicalist versions. Well-known writers associated with these strains are, respectively, Josiah Warren, Michael Bukunin, Peter Kropotkin, Pierre-Joseph Proudhon, and Eugene Debs. Anarcho-syndicalism, for instance, rejects all state politics; democratic producer groups form the hub of anarcho-syndicalist society. Rather than on these literatures, I'm relying on a more applied literature with a distinctively American perspective. All of the points given in this section are discussed in that literature, for example, in Kelly (2001) and Korton (2001).

"A business corporation is organized and carried on primarily for the profit of the stockholders. The powers of the directors are to be employed for that end." So ruled the 1919 Michigan Supreme Court case of *Dodge v. Ford Motor Co.* The purpose of the corporation, especially since the days of the robber barons, has been to maximize stockholder profits. Yet the range of duties of stockholders has declined over the years, for example, even liability long being limited. Little is left beyond mining wealth from the corporation.

It is a legal fiction that the stockholders *are* the corporation. Only habit and a restricted view of the nature of wealth make the exalted role of the stockholder appear to be common sense. There are at least two ways of understanding the corporation. One is as property. On this view, the corporation is something that can be owned. There is arbitrariness in designating stockholders as the exclusive owners, however. On another view and following the work of Coase (1988), the corporation is understood as a nexus of contracts for rights—rather than something that is owned. The stockholders, on this view, are designated to receive all of the residual profits. The oddity in the first view of the corporation is the adjective "exclusive" in the ownership; in the second, the oddity is in "all" of the residual profits. Others contribute substantially to the wealth of the corporation, like the employees and the community.

The property view of understanding the corporation does not entail, however, that owners should be able to do whatever they want with their chunk of property, regardless of the impact on anyone else. In practical terms, it is reckless to allow people to do whatever they want with their property, including wreaking grievous and unethical harm on individuals and society. Should I be free to drive my own private car—my very own property—on the centerline of the road?

Kelly (2001) points out that a corporate leader may refer to her employees as the corporation's greatest asset, and that this is especially true in a knowledge economy. Yet the objective of the corporation, trying to maximize stockholders' profits, is to minimize payments to employees. (Time for play: imagine a possible world where profit is distributed in proportion to each person's contribution to increasing the wealth of the corporation.)

No, I'm not denying that some companies have profit sharing and other sweet market-governed deals. Yet, perhaps because corporations are regarded as property, it is not surprising that employees should be treated as things—things on an accounting ledger, things to be outsourced, things that cost. No, I'm not denying that humans have rights, for example, against racial and gender discrimination. Yet it is surprising that a politically free people would permit employees to depend upon market forces to govern matters of employee privacy, unreasonable searches and seizure, and due process. Employees have no *right* to a say in corporate governance.

It is often said that, ironically, corporations are designated as artificial *persons*. These persons enjoyed some human rights, and still do. In its *Santa Clara* decision in 1886, for instance, the United

States Supreme Court ruled that a corporation is an artificial person. So corporations enjoyed protections under the First, Fourth, and Fourteenth Amendments, like *humans*. Recognizing corporations as persons gave corporations more rights than some humans, such as African-Americans. Hold that thought!

Modern corporations no longer have any public purpose, in contrast to earlier practice. Their purposes are entirely private. Further, the community has no ownership stake in the corporation, and a corporation can happily relocate from Michigan to Mexico or to Mongolia.

Marjorie Kelly (2001) claims that the divine right of kings has been succeeded by the divine right of capital. She makes a comparison of shareholders with feudal nobility, who expected and who received excess returns for doing very little. The king owned his kingdom and his people, and she argues that ownership conferred a right to govern. She suggests that in corporate practice, for instance, there is a predemocratic concept of liberty reserved for property owners. Kelly argues that a principal discrimination suffered in American life—exemplified in the practices of the corporation—is wealth discrimination.

Rebeginnings

Democratization of the economic system and of corporations requires symbolic analysis at the deepest societal level. The wavering line of pressure and counterpressure (to use Burke's words again) is not likely to shift without rhetorical analysis.

For economies as a whole, turn again to applied American literature on the democratization of the economic system. Michael Albert (2003), for instance, suggests *Parecon*, participatory economics. Its central organizational components are "social rather than private ownership; nested worker and consumer councils and balanced job complexes rather than corporate workplace organization; remuneration for effort and sacrifice rather than for property, power, or output; participatory planning rather than markets or central planning; and participatory self-management rather than class rule" (Albert, 2003, 84).

For corporations, Kelly (2001) and Korton (2001) both make the important point that reform is a systemic problem, and that a change of consciousness is needed. Kelly proposes requiring corporations to have a public (as well as a private) purpose and to renew their charters every twenty years, with the decision influenced by community impact statements. Another way to work toward this is the German practice of codetermination that guarantees board seats on corporations to employees.

Yet, without attention to the symbolic, no desirable change in consciousness can be expected and no serious systemic adjustments can be expected to fly. Conversely, given the right attention to the symbolic, dynamics implicated in globalization are likely over the years to encourage such consciousness change.

Recall the cloacal symbolic level, discussed in Essay 14. Remember Laporte's claim (1993, 77) that being civilized, being cleaned, requires a master. Remember Freud's claim that cleanliness, order, and beauty are marks of civilization.

The "civilizing" process is what-counts-as-civilizing, and it is hard for a person within a particular version of a civilizing process to give the time of day to what is not counted-from-within-her-particular-version as civilized. Forms of cleanliness are critical for designating someone or something as civilized. So Laporte contrasts the "ancient" Roman and "ancient" Irish concepts of what-counts-as-civilization. She speaks of O'Donovan's *Irish Annales* of the soon-to-be-king Aedh. To make a symbolic point, Aedh knowingly drank from priestly sewage. Explains Laporte, the "legitimacy of power has its foundations in the shit of the clergy. The mouth of power swallows the shit of God himself. . . ." (Laporte, 1993, 110). During Laporte's description, you and I experience genuine repugnance and disgust at Aedh's version of what-counts-as-civilization; but the repugnance and disgust is also genuinely socially constructed.

Symbolically, the economic master is clean. It is only the master who displays cleanliness, order, and beauty. Even nowadays, people who want to succeed in the office choose to wear power suits—perhaps to manifest cleanliness, order, and beauty.

Symbolically and by contrast, the employee is dirty. He or she is disorderly and ugly. He is "trailer trash." I am not suggesting that employees do have these features; I am speaking of the symbolic that operates at the unconscious level. In earlier times it was easy to pick out the workers. They dressed distinctively; they looked like workers; employees were often physically *unclean*. As general living standards have risen, it is now harder to identify employees—and body odor is no longer normal. In the United States at least, workers have now been renamed middle-class, and they work at office-type jobs as well as at manual labor. But the symbolic residue remains in our psyches. It is uncivilized, symbolically, to grant power to workers that in the symbolic world remain as if unclean.

The truth is that a prerequisite to economic enlightenment is not a cleaning up of employees; rather, it's a cleaning up of symbolic baggage. Governance practice as art should include driving a stake through misleading economic symbols, like those of the invisible hand and the corporation as an artificial person.

> To found a great empire for the sole purpose of raising up a people of customers, may at first sight appear a project fit only for a nation of shopkeepers. It is, however, a project altogether unfit for a nation of shopkeepers; but extremely fit for a nation that is governed by shopkeepers.
>
> —*Adam Smith*

16 • A Nun and Barbed Wire

The art of governance should recognize the barbs in systems and the pivotal role of society in creating the barbed wire. Barbed wire, symbolizing the combination of beneficial and hurtful effect, is discussed in terms of prevalence, types, and unraveling. Immigration and Corrections are examples.

> This comes from dangling from the ceiling–
> I'm goitered like a Lombard cat.
>
> . . . .
>
> Loins concertina'd in my gut,
> I drop an arse as counterweight
> and move without the help of eyes.
>
> . . . .
>
> Defend my labor's cause,
> good Giovanni, from all strictures:
> I live in hell and paint its pictures.
>
> —*Michelangelo Buonarroti*

> It was a nun they say invented barbed wire.
>
> —*James Joyce*

She had suffered a long history of sexual assaults. Even though she had clearly identified her attackers, the result of the barbed wire is that the police made no arrests. Reports the *Clinical Society News,* "She shares her past with no trace of anger, but the residue of fear persists. When in public she looks around anxiously. She looks apologetic when she speaks, almost as though she feels undeserving of someone's attention, as though it were a gift she didn't deserve" (Crosby, 2003, 5). The report goes on to explain that she is transsexual. Being a person-in-herself in-her-difference in this case includes the complainant (bureaucratic term) being in limbo between a body with male and a transformed body with female appendages. She dresses like a woman and is receiving hormone treatments, but she has not yet had the operation that will realize her goal of becoming a woman.

Should the barb in the response, or nonresponse, to this person be conceptualized simply as a *police matter?* Certainly it is a police matter, and I agree that the police should take personal responsibility for what they did and did not do. But I think that it is society's barbed wire. Society has a pivotal role in constructing and staffing governance systems and arrangements, or the lack of them. These systems then sculpt the character of system functionaries, like the system of painting (see quote above) that sculpted Michelangelo's body. I go further and suggest that the barbed wire manifested in such governance systems is part of society's dreams. Unconsciously for many members, I think that that community wants the victim to be sexually assaulted; correction—it wants to sexually assault her. As Michelangelo writes (see Bonner, 2004), "I live in hell, and paint its pictures."

The art of governance should ignore neither the barbs in its systems nor the decisive role of society in creating the barbed wire. Practice as art should assume responsibility not only for its own systems but also for the society that wants the systems. It should include conceptualizing governance, with its barbs, not only as a manifestation of society's consciousness but also of its unconscious. The barbed wire manifested in governance systems is part of society's dreams. The public and private bureaucrat should see herself not merely as following superior orders, hooked to a paycheck or to a profit. Like Shakespeare's Henry V, she can aspire to be a maker of fashion—a maker of society. "We are the makers of manners, Kate" (*Henry V,* 5, 2, 280). No official should be a mere functionary. She should be, at least, one of society's therapists. For this, practice as art includes understanding of the psychological, including social psychology.

In this essay, I comment on the prevalence of barbs and describe three types of governance context that exhibit barbed wire. By speaking of barbed wire, I am pointing toward what is painful and controlling in governance systems. Barbed wire has a quality that is often exhibited by a system—or a program, a policy, an agency, an individual. As I have explained before, it is a quality of compulsion, of force. It is deployed for what the practitioner—like the rancher—considers to be a useful purpose. It controls, limits. It can hurt; it can dig into the flesh. At a minimum, it denies passage. It serves (as in "services") to keep them in (e.g., as in "corrections services"), or to keep them out (e.g., as in "immigration and naturalization services"). It is impersonal, harsh, and metallic (iron as in "cage")—either in the flesh or metaphorically. I borrow the term "barbed wire" from an anecdote in James Joyce's *Ulysses,* his account of a Dubliner's odyssey. Joyce (1997, 147–148) speaks of the nice nun with the really sweet face. He describes this nice nun, and then he concludes with a sentence that continues to fascinate me. "It was a nun they say invented barbed wire."

Claiming that barbed wire in governance systems is part of society's dreams is jolting. So was his nun for Joyce. His nun has a really sweet face, and Joyce thinks (and so do I) that she is good society. But it was such "good society" who invented barbed wire that hurts even as it helps. That strikes Joyce as paradoxical, and I think that he is referring to the much-discussed philosophico-theological "problem" of the perfectly good, omniscient, omnipotent, and loving God, who creates a world that—wow!—contains pain. However, I am referring to the humbler problem of good society *wanting* governance barbs.

Prevalence of Barbed Wire

Governance institutions do many of society's dirty jobs. Governance systems execute not only what-is-counted-as-civilized (see Essay 14) but also what is *not.* Burrell (1997) suggests that Taylorism was about controlling the peasants, for instance. For societies embracing democratic ideals, conscious and unconscious desires can be achieved by pushing decision-making down into the public and private bureaucracies—and then repressing the undemocratic implications. Recall the example of the independent U.S. Federal Reserve System, which can be described as protecting business community interests against the vagaries of democracy, for example, fighting inflation by sustaining unemployment. Pushing decision-making down into the State Department can achieve barbed-wire objectives, like decades of punishing Vietnam for the military insult of the Vietnam War. Intelligence agencies are buried even deeper, where dirty hands and even the budget can be shielded by the cloak of national security.

Barbed wire is not an isolated institutional phenomenon, limited to the sorts of examples just given. On the contrary, it seems to be everywhere—and it persists. Here is a lead story from the *New York Times,* and recall that there are said to be excellent treatments available for most of the patients I am going to mention.

> Hundreds of patients released from state psychiatric hospitals in New York in recent years are being locked away on isolated floors of nursing homes, where they are barred from going outside on their own, have almost no contact with others and have little ability to contest their confinement. . . . (Levy, 2002, 1)

Writes James Joyce (1997, 35), "History . . . is a nightmare from which I am trying to awake."

This is excessive hurt. But even in the best of circumstances, the society through the governance system embraces barbed wire that hurts as it helps. This evokes the idea of *pharmakon.* Jacques Derrida explains that pharmakon signifies drug, denoting both remedy and poison. Similarly, the remedy of the system is unavailable without the barbed wire. Derrida is commenting on Plato's *Phaedrus,* which discusses the virtues of writing and reason over, respectively, speech and myth. (Such a discussion nowadays could be about the virtues of the e-book over the traditional book.) Michel Foucault (1977a) also writes of pharmakon in analyzing the shift to modern "lenient" punishment from pre–nineteenth-century punishment that inflicted horrendous torture directly upon the body. The target now is not the body but the thought, the will, the inclination. When an execution approaches, Foucault reports that the patient is injected with tranquilizers. He could have added that also the rectal orifice is plugged so that a side effect of death from electrocution will not soil the scene. Modern punishment, for him, is both cure and poison. He points out that we punish, but it is "a way of saying" that we want to obtain a cure.

In reflecting on barbed wire, let's stay with criminal corrections. Reflect on our guilty foreknowledge of the prevalence of the forcible rape of men and women within prison walls. Correctional *service,* a euphemism for a service that contains barbed wire!

It's reasonable that many of us want bad people to be stored in a Spartan manner, in stir. No eggs Benedict, for example, behind bars at Sunday brunch! But your and my guilty knowledge of the prevalence of forcible rapes within the walls reflects badly on you and me—to the extent that our foreknowledge makes us responsible for these atrocities. Arguably, it's state-sponsored rape to the extent that the sentencing authorities know that it will happen and to the extent that they have the power to stop it and do not. Ironically, and as evidence that it can be stopped, it doesn't happen on death row.

"This legislation is the first serious federal attempt to deal with a human rights crisis that has been virtually ignored in this country," states Lara Stemple (2002) who heads Stop Prison Rape (SPR). The Prison Rape Reduction Act was introduced in 2002 in the U.S. Senate. It seeks to study the extent of the problem and aims to create a program of standards and incentives to help correctional officers prevent prison rape of men and women. Only 2002! Stephen Donaldson claimed in 1993 that 290,000 males are sexually assaulted each year in prisons. He wrote (Donaldson, 1993) that, "The catastrophic experience of sexual violence usually extends beyond a single incident, often becoming a daily assault. . . ."

This is not an isolated barb. Correctional agencies display many barbarous barbs. I have visited perhaps fifteen or so prisons and penitentiaries in my life. That's not much; but I hope that our society is not being graded on the way it treats its prisoners. The lunacy begins in precorrections—with the sentencing. Why do we incarcerate more people, and for longer periods, than does any

other advanced country? Let's suspend the country club privileges
of the rational and intelligent judge who, rather than resign, sentenced Leandro Andrade to fifty years for a $153.54 misdemeanor!
How judicial was the Chicago judge who sentenced a multiple
murderer to more than a thousand years? No, the prisoner was not
Mr. Methuselah, and the judge was reportedly sober. Why do we
tolerate the prosecutorial blackmail involved in plea bargaining?

Types

Let's turn to three contexts of barbed wire. Surely others will prefer an alternative set of categories, for example, including
underbarbed.

Context 1: Naturally Barbed

It's hard to think of a barbless military or a barbless police *force*.
Sometimes being barbed is much of what it's about. For the purposes of this category, we needn't worry about the truth or falsity
of the claim that all government is legitimately backed by force.
There are enough obvious examples to avoid that. Even these obvious cases can be overbarbed, of course. A military can have more
means of violence than humanity needs, like an excess of biological, chemical, and atomic weaponry; and a police force can exert
more violence than human and situational considerations dictate,
as reflected in the ritual of handcuffing even when handcuffing is
unnecessary. Being barbed appropriately is not the same as being
hyperbarbed.

Context 2: Barbarously Barbed

To the extent that I am responsible for it or to the extent that I
approve of it, a barbarously barbed-wire agency is one that makes
me ethically ugly. Correctional services constitute one example,
fencing in. Immigration service is also at some point in this spectrum of agencies that are overbarbed, fencing out.

Ask former customers of the Immigration and Naturalization

Service (INS), when they have finally escaped the control of INS. Ellis Island attitudes still reign, I think they will whisper. I recall when I first came to the United States—in 1958. I came by train from Montreal to New York. Two Immigration and Naturalization Service officers came into the car of the train, collecting the passports and sitting about half way down. A female passenger, very well dressed, attempted to go to the bathroom: "Sit down!" came the sharp command. She turned tail and walked back to her seat. Then I overheard one of the officers exclaim to the other in a booming voice, waving a passport and pointing to another passenger in the train car: "This belongs to the [racial epithet for a Spanish person] over there." At that time, I didn't know the word (never heard it before); but I did recognize the hostility. No contact with the INS in later years was ever absent verbal harassment and denigration, including every step of the naturalization process. "Hurry up! Hurry up! Or you will have to start the process all over again some other day," exclaims one official. That was enough decades ago. Maybe times have now changed; conversations with some current applicants disabuse me of that hope. "I'm now going to test to see whether you can speak English; read this," says another official, apparently oblivious of the fact that the previous conversation had been in English. "My name is Mr. Rosa. I am a man," reads the text of the assigned book. "Good! Now I am going to test to see if you can write English. Write a sentence," instructs the official. "I am a man," I write.

Context 3: Unspeakably Barbed

Far from the naturally barbed end of the spectrum, barbed wire conjures up the image of a totally inhuman type of barbed wire— the wire of the concentration camp. It is too mild to say that this is at the extreme of an array of contexts of barbed wire; it is off the end of any scale. We can understand Theodor Adorno (1981, 34); "To write poetry after Auschwitz is barbaric."

The administrative outlines of the Final Solution, as you know, were settled at a meeting on January 20, 1942, at Wannsee, a villa near Berlin. How could a group of fourteen such rational and intelligent people consent to such an unspeakably barbed, totally inhuman and inhumane project? This question is fleshed out by Kenneth Branagh and others in the brilliant made-for-TV movie (with an inelegant, albeit accurate, title) *Conspiracy*. The movie recounts the Wannsee meeting. Kenneth Branagh plays the meeting chair, Gen. Reinhard Heydrich; Stanley Tucci (also brilliant) acts the part of the meeting's secretary, Adolf Eichmann. The other participants are respected officials from affected governmental agencies, like the Foreign Office.

Heydrich runs the meeting with consummate administrative skill. He shows courtesy and deference to other viewpoints; at times he calls for refreshments to defuse tensions; he proceeds relentlessly toward the already settled goal. Later, the actor Branagh (2004) commented that, "Playing him, I felt that had he been asked to eradicate Eskimos, cabinet-makers or gymnasts, he would have proceeded in the same way, with the same relentless soulless quality." For me, the high point in the movie is when the meeting has broken up and only two are left in the room. Eichmann puts on the adagio from Schubert's Quintet in C Major. The second person is visibly transformed into the world of the sublime, and Eichmann comments "Tears your heart out, doesn't it?" Long pause—and Eichmann sneers, "I don't understand that sentimental Viennese shit."

Art in Unraveling Barbed Wire

Joseph F. Glidden's invention of literal barbed wire in 1873 led to a storm of controversy. In fact, the opponents came to call it *the Devil's Rope*. I favor attention no less intense about barbed wire in governance. I prefer practice as art that reflects overall understanding rather than case-by-case arguments considering this situation (e.g., corrections) and then that (e.g., immigration).

An overall understanding of barbed wire should focus on society rather than limiting itself to a particular governance function. It should connect that focus with a larger theoretical framework about society. Many will agree that the barbed wire is connected with modernity's rationalizing project—a perverse and unintended outcome. Preferences will vary about which frameworks and thinkers can help in carrying the interpretation to a more interesting depth.

Did governance invent barbed wire, you might ask; or did barbed wire in society invent governance, reflecting society's image? Does the barbed wire of our set of institutions like the U.S. Post Office —with its delivery of junk mail at discount rates—come from society? Or, vice versa? I agree that it's a two-way street. But I imagine that the nature of the barbed wire in governance originates in the conscious and unconscious barbed wire in society.

It's parallel to the nice nun with the really sweet face. Wasn't Joyce's nun largely socially created, and didn't she then influence society? I imagine that the barbed wire in governance and in bureaucracy can be understood only by paying attention to the sources of the barbed wire in society; I suppose that the discourse of society is decisive. "It was a nun they say invented barbed wire." Let the art of governance engage more fully the good society that wants barbed wire!

17 • Love and Mere Efficiency

The post-traditional practitioner should be motivated as a regulative ideal by love rather than by mere efficiency. It should embrace unengineering as a symbol.

Bureaucracy develops the more perfectly, the more it is "dehumanized," the more completely it succeeds in eliminating from official business love, hatred, and all the purely personal, irrational and emotional elements which escape calculation.

—*Max Weber*

The heart has its reasons of which the head knows nothing.

—*Blaise Pascal*

In an act of love, the Masai people in June 2002 gave the United States fourteen cows for the affected people of New York. The Masai had just heard about September 11. At first the State Department accepted the cows. Then it had second thoughts. It thought of difficulties like health hazards and said that it wanted to sell the cows for local jewelry. Finally the State Department realized that its "sophisticated" response was not as human as the Masai's gesture of love.

Contrast that with stories about efficiency in Sam's Club and Toys "R" Us. The policy of Sam's Club, a Wal-Mart subsidiary, was to lock some overnight shift workers inside stores, an efficient way to protect stores from theft by employees and outsiders.

The *New York Times* reports a manager saying that "Wal-Mart is like any other company. They're concerned about the bottom line, and the bottom line is affected by shrinkage in the store" (Greenhouse, 2004, 1). It adds that another reason for lock-ins is "to increase efficiency—workers could not sneak outside to smoke a cigarette, get high or make a quick trip home." It tells the story of Michael Rodriguez, who crushed an ankle while an overnight shift worker. Rodriguez had to wait an hour before being transported to a hospital; there was no on-duty manager with a key. Toys "R" Us is reported in another *New York Times* story to be seeking efficiency by altering some hourly workers' time records, one manager "secretly deleting hours to cut their paychecks and to fatten his store's bottom line" (Greenhouse, 2004a, 1). The story reports that Family Dollar and Pep Boys have been sued for deleting hours and that settlements were reached with two Kinko's centers for erasing time for thirteen workers.

The post-traditional practitioner is, and should be, motivated as a regulative ideal by love. I'm suggesting that she should not stick *merely* with efficiency as a regulative ideal for motivation. Post-traditional governance is, and should be, fueled by love for the regulative ideal of, like Romeo for Juliet and vice versa, *love for each whole person-in-herself in-her-difference.*

Such a *regulative ideal* is a vision or benchmark of what should be done even though it might be, on a consistent or frequent basis, *impossible.* Examples of other regulative ideals include the political, such as Jean-Jacques Rousseau's "general will"—and even *efficiency* itself. They are impossible to achieve always and completely. On a personal level, there are life-enriching regulative sets of ideals that include impossibly high standards and impossible combinations like "Turn the other cheek" and "Don't tread on me." Striving to reach a regulative ideal that is impossible, I try, I fail, I half succeed, I lapse, I try again.

Taking love as a motivation does imply taking Max Weber seriously: see the quote above from him (and also Essay 3) about dehumanizing bureaucracy. It also implies taking seriously those like Marcuse (1991) and others like Helen Caldicott (2002), who warn against the warfare economy. The implications will ruffle feathers.

Some will be disturbed by Caldicott's description of "corporate madness and death merchants," for example, and they may be concerned at her suggestion that "the Pentagon needs to be virtually dismantled" (Caldicott, 2002, 186). It hardly helps to recall President Eisenhower's January 1961 warning that, "In the councils of government, we must guard against the acquisition of unwarranted influence, whether sought or unsought, by the military-industrial complex. The potential for the disastrous rise of misplaced power exists and will persist. We must never let the weight of this combination endanger our liberties or democratic process." The draft of Eisenhower's speech used the adjectives, not military-industrial, but military-industrial-congressional. The intensity of such difficulties suggests the desirability of including attention to rhetoric, focusing on such options as unengineering.

Personal Love

Love in governance should include a focus on the individual person, even if that focus is a tall order—as it is. Love for nobody should be nobody's idea of loving; Roland Barthes (1978, 74) is right to remind us that "No one wants to speak of love unless it is for someone." Such a focus involves relating to the individual person in her uniqueness. It is a being-with, a caring-for, the individual whole person, warts and all.

Love in governance appears paradoxical only if governance is understood as business as usual. Love as motivation does involve a contradiction if love is understood as extending out to the individual person while governance is seen as limited to rules-for-groups. Or, to put it another way, love in governance is oxymoronic if at root it welcomes poetic or spiritual freedom while governance does not. Governance motivated by love does want to shift away from viewing governance as rule-making-for-groups and rule-application-to-groups. It moves toward focusing on the individual and on poetic or spiritual freedom.

It is a shift toward what does happen now in some governance contexts today—in exceptions. Most of us have encountered these exceptions. Some individuals and some groups author them, with varying degrees of frequency and intensity. Weren't there examples on September 11—and before? Examples are sometimes described under different names, for example, gifting (Cunningham & Schneider, 2001). Individual-focused love can pop up or pop down. The choice is not between the extremes of either permanently on-going loving or no loving at all. A movement from efficiency toward love as a motivation can include aiming at increasing the incidence of poppings up.

Practical challenges are presented by this understanding of love and governance, however. Consider one—the "excessive" feature of love. Love at full throttle is a force so mountainous, so "Wagnerian," that it invites talk about the sublime. Diane Ackerman offers one account of female erotic love in terms of horses (1995, 196–217), for example, and of male erotic love in terms of racing cars (1995, 217–227). Consider another challenge, talking about exceeding group rules and group structures. Not all rules are bad, for example, children without rules often fail. An enterprise metastasized with group rules, living and breathing standard operating procedures, is a different matter. Visit any large organization. Aren't the clients of managers groups of individuals, whether employees or members of the public? I think so. People are sometimes treated as humans-in-themselves in-their-differences. Aren't they exceptions, pop-ups?

Unengineering

Love has to surmount the rhetorical weight of competitor symbolic systems—efficiency-in-capitalism and patriarchy. I suggest that the art of governance could inch toward love-as-a-motivation through introduction of such countersymbols as *unengineering*.

Both private and public agencies and officials have been conditioned by, and are used to, an efficiency ethic. Efficiency's huge rhetorical mass results from "efficiency" being part of the dominant system of symbols and rhetoric that attend and support the capitalist ethic. Capitalism has been characterized, as mentioned, as the rational pursuit of ever more wealth (i.e., Max Weber, 1958, 17). It privileges economic efficiency as a value, and efficiency is a central idea in economic theory (see Essay 15).

Efficiency's rhetorical mass exceeds the weight of its rational support in that efficiency as a concept is, for instance, artificial and arbitrary. It is artificial in the sense of being socially constructed. Practitioners often notice that what cannot be counted tends to be excluded from benefit-cost analyses. It is arbitrary in the sense that what is efficient from one perspective often is inefficient from another, and that a coherent concept of efficiency that considers all perspectives would be a political compromise. For example, a steel mill may be highly efficient from the perspective of a company's bottom line; yet simultaneously it may be inefficient from the ecological perspective. I remember reflecting about this distinction as I drove through the pollution of the hardworking steel mills in Gary, Indiana.

Talk about love also runs against society's patriarchal grain, the logic of symbolic systems like that of patriarchy. Look at bell hooks's third book on love. Writes bell hooks, "In the patriarchal male imagination, the subject of love was relegated to the realm of the weak and was replaced by narratives of power and domination. . . . Love became solely women's work" (hooks, 2002, 77). Earlier, she writes that, "Patriarchy has always seen love as women's work, degraded and devalued labor" (hooks, 2002, xviii).

What is wanted, importantly, are new symbols like unengineering. Unengineering entails relinquishing symbols or nostrums like reengineering to the extent that they do not embrace love for the individual. Reengineering stands for techniques *motivated* inward toward the needs and functioning of the organization. Even when focusing on outward relationships, the primary interest is inward. Reengineering, successor to total quality management, is defined by Loh (1997, xiv) as "a multidisciplinary approach to implementing fundamental change in the way work is performed across the organization with the goal of dramatically improving performance and stakeholder value." Morris and Brandon point out that reengineering has been given various names like streamlining, restructuring, transformation, and restructuring, and they add (1993, 6) that "regardless of the name, the goal is almost always the same: increased ability to compete through cost reduction." Champy (1995, 34) describes reengineering thoughts as being about "What is this business for? What kind of culture do we want? How do we do our work? What kind of people do we want to work with?" And Fincham asserts (2000, 174) that "Business Process Reengineering (BPR) appeals to managers essentially as a means of control over the many vicissitudes of organization life, and there can be little doubt that to many it must seem like a necessary charm against the dark forces of competition and failure." The point of all these examples is that reengineering here is taken as symbolizing approaches that are primarily motivated *inward*.

Unengineering is directed toward knowing and embracing love. It seeks to foster the attitudes and behavior of love, from the inside toward the outside of the organization. Unengineering's epistemology should correspond to its loving goal. It should be radically open not only to the brain but also to the heart: see the quote from Pascal, above. Martha Nussbaum (1990, 262) tells us that knowledge "of the heart must come from the heart—from and in its pains and longings, its emotional responses." Intellectualism is not enough. She "insists that knowledge of love is not a state or function of the solitary person at all, but a complex way of being, feeling, and interacting with another person" (Nussbaum, 1990, 274).

Unengineering asks governance to reorient itself *outward* to the individual-in-herself in-her-difference. Recall Essay 15 on the public service element in private corporations, an element that was usual in corporate charters in colonial America and in the earlier years of the United States. Unengineering's aim is to go beyond exclusive focus on benefiting the agency. Or to put it in a slogan for practice as art, unengineering calls for the death of mere efficiency.

18 • To Kill the King, and "Good and No Places"

This essay speaks of an ideal (or ideology) of opening democracy. It talks of a citizen turn. This is illustrated in terms of political hierarchy, noting that both hierarchical democracy and open democracy present aporia. Resymbolization is suggested to nourish the impulse that the existence of hierarchy is not the norm that needs no evidence, but a deviation that requires justification. Executing the king requires changing symbolic systems in citizens' heads.

> What we need, however, is a political philosophy that
> isn't erected around the problem of sovereignty, nor
> therefore around the problems of law and prohibition.
> We need to cut off the King's head; in political theory
> that has still to be done.
>
> —*Foucault*

> For I agree with you that there is a natural aristocracy
> among [*sic*] men. The grounds of this are virtue and
> talents. . . . There is also an artificial aristocracy
> founded on wealth and birth, without either
> virtue or talents.
>
> —*Thomas Jefferson*

Thomas Hobbes's *Leviathan* can be read as symbolic of seeking citizen-citizen salvation from what he considered necessary political hierarchy. Published in 1651, Hobbes's *Leviathan* started from the citizen and would have citizens trade their radical insecurity—

their "state of warre"—at the price of subjection to the king. He writes of the "great Leviathan . . . or Mortall God" (Hobbes, 1991, 120). Hobbes's citizens sought their well-being, not from themselves and within their relationship to their fellow citizens, but from a political authority above. Hobbes seeks citizen happiness from a king or equivalent power.

Stand Hobbes on his head! Realize the ideal of each person, not the king, as the great Leviathan . . . or Mortall God! This ideal is the primacy of each whole person-in-herself in-her-difference. Progress toward this upending has been made. Many countries, including Hobbes's, have hierarchical democracy. In many, this hierarchy has become less steep. I sympathize with Foucault's claim above about cutting off the king's head, however. Many royal trappings remain, even in republics.

The post-traditional practitioner should aim toward *opening democracy*. The emphasis should be on the process of a citizen turn rather than on the end states. I was planning to suggest this emphasis on the process of opening democracy as a civic religion, as that suggests the faith and fervor I have in mind. But I choose not to, because that can easily transform into system (or constitution) worship or mere nationalism. It is better to think of it as a kind of ideology.

In the first section, I start with Hobbes in order to speak of the language that underlies the hierarchical and the open. The second section points to the significant problems that attend hierarchical democracy no less than open democracy. Talking of end-states encounters aporia. In the third section, I speak of a citizen turn and antecedents in political thought. The burden of proof should be shifted from the lateral to the hierarchical. Resymbolization is required to nourish the impulse that the existence of hierarchy is not the norm that needs no evidence, but a deviation that requires justification. Executing the king, piece by piece, entails changing the language that is in the citizen's head.

The Hierarchy of Traditional Language

Start with Hobbes's choices (a kind of Hobson's choice), and then turn to hierarchy. This subtitle contains a weak pun. One meaning is the nature of hierarchy within traditional language, for example, of sovereign, law, and limit. Another is the sovereignty of traditional language itself.

Hierarchy in Hobbes is established under the appearance—illusion, delusion—that the act of establishing political hierarchy is nonhierarchical. I agree that a hierarchy with such a fairy tale has advantages over another hierarchy that is established on a frankly hierarchical basis, like the divine right of kings or the natural right of wealth. Hobbes did a service in advocating his extremely steep hierarchy on the basis of a social contract between each and every person and then with the king, a social contract that beyond the world of his imaginative geometry never happened and never could have happened.

Leviathan begins with excellent philosophical flourish. Yet, with that lack of sympathy that comes from living in a different time period and in a different world, students nowadays are apt to be bemused by what follows—the now-uninspiring political conclusions that Hobbes reached. The ruling boss—king or parliament limited in his day to wealthy landowners—in Hobbes's system, has absolute power over subjects who have made a social contract to turn over all liberties to the boss. The sovereign has absolute power over subjects as long as s/he is successful in keeping them alive.

"Why are we being required to read Hobbes's *Leviathan*?" a student asked the other day. My answer spoke of Hobbes's contribution to the development of political thought (a "flowering and a seedbed" as Michael Oakeshott put it) and of the issue of government in times of exceptional fear, and the student appeared satisfied. But I wasn't. I should have made it clearer that each of us, including you and me, always think within the constraints of our available language. Hobbes's freedom to theorize was trapped by the symbolization within which he thought. The genius of Hobbes is that he was able to make such interesting advances at the edges of his available paradigm. But his language limited his world.

"The limits of my language are the limits of my world." So writes Ludwig Wittgenstein (1961, 56). This applies no less in a field like political theory, like governance. The limits of my (and your) symbolization are the limits of my (and your) capability of killing the king.

Hobbes faced limits at the conscious as well as the unconscious levels. Consciously it worried Hobbes that King Charles II, restored to the throne after the English Civil War, might be angry at the individualistic basis on which the hierarchy, the monarchy, was justified in *The Leviathan.* Hobbes is said to have taken up a position at the side of a London street where he believed that the king would pass in his sedan chair. Hobbes bowed when the king's chair came into view, and he was mightily relieved when the king greeted him warmly. Phew! That was a close one!

More significant were the unconscious limits. I imagine that Hobbes's acceptance of the need for hierarchy was radically unconscious. How could he not have absorbed hierarchy as an assumption from all aspects of his particular childhood and later life? He worked for a powerful lord; he lived in top-down times; his daddy had been a minor cleric, given to anger and always looking up (and down); and so on.

Our available way of looking at the world is captured in the symbolic system of signs that constitute language, operating mainly through the unconscious. Language is understood here as discourse as the latter term is described in Essay 6. Language has a narrow sense, a matter of syntax and grammar and the literary rest. But I mean the broad sense of encompassing a person's (or a field's) sense of an acceptable way of looking at the world and an acceptable way of doing things. Such a language has parameters. These parameters have definite benefits; but, analyses being confined within them, they are also disabling.

There are many kinds and hues of hierarchy. Yet the language(s) of governance do not contain a rich set of symbols, signs, and concepts for the varieties and nuances of *hierarchy.* We are funneled in talk about hierarchy, and the shades of meaning tend to be lost. Thinkers can, and should, coin new words or symbols. But the new symbols always face an uphill struggle against the pressure of the *logic* of the symbolic systems implicated in traditional language. This complaint is similar to that mentioned in Essay 15 about capitalism.

For a start, here are two perspectives, or overlapping senses, of hierarchy in society. They are what I will call the institutional and the comprehensive, and my view is that governance action as art should have primary concern with the comprehensive. As the name implies, the former understands hierarchy from the perspective of the institutional, the political or economic or administrative system. The institutional in politics could speak of the structure of participation and discourse, and the like. The most dramatic example of the institutional is the bureaucratic, (mis)conceived as a matter of structure and charts. It's a chief flea on the back of a deputy chief flea, being on the back of an assistant deputy chief flea, being on another flea's back, and down to the back of the lowest flea in the hierarchy. I don't want to be dismissive of the institutional, however. In the wake of a post-traditional thinker like Mary Parker Follett, for example, the possibility of establishing temporary networks of arrangements is exciting for many. They would be even more attractive if they aimed for, say, what Michel Foucault (1977, xiii–xiv) advised. A network of nodes could aim for actions that "prefer what is positive and multiple, difference over uniformity" and "mobile arrangements over systems."

The comprehensive view recognizes hierarchy from the perspective of the individual-in-herself in-her-difference in society. It focuses on practices from the perspective of an individual who possesses a combination and changing array of characteristics. It's against domination that treats a specific individual like a minority or aged person as subordinate, as less than she could and should be. It's against making a particular other fit into my mold. But it is from the perspective of a person whose characteristics are not fixed. It's against a static view of a human's identity. I am still attracted to the comment by Nancy Fraser (1991, 99) that "no one is simply a woman: one is rather, for example, a white, Jewish, middle-class woman, a philosopher, lesbian, a socialist, and a mother. Moreover, since everyone acts in a plurality of contexts, the different descriptions comprising any individual's social identity fade in and out of focus. Thus, one is not always a woman in the same degree. . . ."

End-State Regulative Ideals: Good and No Places

Reflect on alternative end-state regulative ideals that are *good and no places,* hierarchical democracy and open democracy. "I admit that not a few things in the manners and laws of the Utopians seemed

very absurd to me. . . ." (More, 1949, 82). When coining the term
"utopia," Thomas More was indulging in wordplay that his imaginary island was both a good place and a no place; the prefix "u"
comes from the Greek *eu* meaning "good" as well as from *ou*, meaning "not." More's main character, Raphael Hythlodaeus, sports a
surname that means "well versed in nonsense." And More can end
his utopia—initiating a literary genre—"Yet I must confess that there
are many things in the Utopian Commonwealth that I wish rather
than expect to be followed among our citizens" (More, 1949, 83).

It is false to think that hierarchical democracy is real and practical, and that open democracy is unreal and impractical. By calling these alternative regulative ideals *good and no places,* I want
to say that there is significant obscurity in the ideals of both hierarchical democracy and open democracy. Like in More's Utopia,
both sets of alternatives lead to aporia.

Hierarchical Democracy

The history of the world hitherto has been the history of hierarchy
dominant, although it has included many hundreds of years of hierarchy under siege and eroding. I revel in the achievements and
benefits of representative democracy, even when there is not as
much participatory governance as I would prefer. But we should
remind ourselves of the paradoxes of representative government,
paradoxes that should not be glossed over by platitudes.

In placing in perspective the difficulties in understanding open
governance, it is helpful to contemplate the gaping flaws we tolerate in the hierarchical alternative. For examples in representative
democracy, turn to aggregating citizen preferences and to the problem of silence. These are but two examples.

The polis-centered decision rules of our familiar political hierarchy present a dirty little secret, well described and well repressed.
There is no *right* decision rule in aggregating votes. Different
methods of aggregating preferences can lead to different results,
for example, using the Borda, the Condorcet, the first-past-the-
post, or other decision rules. Then comes Kenneth Arrow's possibility theorem. The theorem demonstrates that no method for

aggregating social preferences can guarantee not to violate even a set of five trivial conditions that Arrow discusses (Arrow, 1963). The conditions are trivial in the sense that they are requirements like "transitivity" (if A is preferred to B and if B is preferred to C, then A is preferred to C). They are not complex notions like fairness or justice. As an ethical enterprise grounded on mere aggregation or even mere consensus, representative democracy is problematic. In a polis-centered system of aggregation, this is something to be swept under the rug.

Our current commonsense hierarchical system cannot accommodate silent preferences, no less real merely because they are silent. The fact of silence undermines the "commonsense" of our representative system. Patricia M. Patterson (2000a, 686) suggests that there is more to silence than the absence of talk. As she writes, "Operationalizing discourse as speech or talking is limiting, but not just because terrains of silence are left without account. . . . To enter into a discourse is to enter the language practices that constitute the mental categories in use, and not merely to enter a conversation by opening one's mouth." Voter silence is more than mere voter nonparticipation; it represents not merely apathy and lack of interest. It has meanings, as Patterson underscores, other than consent or ignorance. Silence hides and reveals, just as voting reveals and hides dreams. For this, there is no unflawed mechanical or other aggregation formula.

Open Democracy

This "good and no place" regulative ideal of open democracy also presents both benefits and aporia. Because we have less or no experience of open democracy, the aporia seems more formidable.

Open democracy, I should reemphasize, requires a different language. In such a democracy, the origin and the terminus of public and private sector governance is the whole individual-in-herself and in-her-difference. In such a new ideology, governmental and other energies are directed—in practice as well as in stated intention—toward each person living her life according to her own lights.

Imagine that open governance occurs when no individual is subject to a hierarchy of unwanted control or coercion. There is formidable difficulty. *Unwanted* hierarchy is a problematic notion, for one thing, as the psychology and social construction of wanting is complex. It is peculiar if, in any society, a person cannot freely choose to be subordinate to another. For example, if adults want to subordinate themselves to employers, why not? If adults want to love, honor, and obey other persons, why not? Yet the difference between free and unfree choice of subordination is complicated by yet another distinction. The latter distinction is between what is wanted and what is really wanted, and people can change their minds about commitments already made. It is not always easy to specify what is freely chosen. For instance, we are told that Anglo-Saxons in A.D. 1000 could choose to enter bondage at times of famine or distress. "No legal document was involved, and the new bondsman would be handed a bill-hook or ox-goad in token of his fresh start in servitude. It was a basic transaction—heads for food. The original old English meaning of lord was 'loaf-giver' " (Lacey and Danziger, 2000, 46–47). This appears less free than the student who chooses (of her own free will?) to prepare herself for service to a corporate employer. By definition, invisible chains are difficult to see.

Speaking of *unavoidable* hierarchy in this context is also odd, because it seems to admit that human nature is not yet adequate for open democracy. Even if opening democracy is a long-term and gradual process, it seems speculative to suppose that this nature can be completely altered. For instance, there is the problem of predators who attempt to injure others. It seems no less "common sense" that children require the benefits of hierarchy. It seems weak to reply that children need hierarchy just as it used to be thought that they require the benefits of being beaten for bad conduct (the paddle in schools, corporal punishment) and that they should have no rights against their parents (unlike jurisdictions where children can sue their parents). Some coercion appears compelling. Or, is it?

A call for political theory to present a full and airtight specification of open democracy, or hierarchical democracy, can be misguided. To the extent that it is philosophical, such theorizing cannot be limited to what is beyond philosophical questioning. The problematic character of open democracy and of anarchism, while real, is a feature no less in any other ideology. Generality and aporia come with the philosophical (and ideological) territory.

Process Regulative Ideal: Opening Democracy

In aiming toward opening democracy, the practitioner as artist should share responsibility for changing the language. A new language is desirable as a constitutive feature of difficult political action, for example, like denying the rights of natural, to artificial, persons.

Citizen Turn

The symbol of a citizen turn, or citizen-ing, seeks to give primary attention in governance to the liberating potential of citizens. Governmental arrangements need not be ignored, however, even though the whole person-in-herself in-her-difference is irreducibly primary.

Citizen-ing could be described, as I have done before, in terms of two classes of visioning. This visioning is in a wide sense where a person envisions her own life, and where her life is a living of that vision. Class 1 is the visioning proffered by living persons for their own way of living, including visioning for societal action in the political, economic, cultural, and other areas considered significant for their living: call it Class 1 visioning. Class 2 visioning is that offered by systems and on behalf of systems. Examples of such systems include our political systems, our economic systems, our legal systems, our health care systems, our welfare systems, our commercial systems, our military systems, our diplomatic systems, our international systems, our systems of alliances, and our systems of education. The vast and powerful political and economic interests are examples of Class 2 visioning or systems—the complex of agencies that constitute the muscle and spin of the various segments of the political and the economic. Citizen-ing refers to living where as many lives as possible are lived without accepting as primary the manipulation and domination of systems and on behalf of systems—where Class 1 visioning is privileged over Class 2 visioning.

A citizen turn can point out that the historical pattern of political and other relationships generally has been hierarchical, with increasing opening of democracy being the exceptional pattern in some geographical areas. Still there is an assumption in favor of the hierarchical; kings, big and small, "appear" to be commonsense. The high-jump bar is much higher for open, than for hierarchical, democracy. Arguably, the reverse could be the new pattern, emphasizing hierarchy-by-exception. Changes would take place over time, and there would be advantages in learning more from experiences in the ongoing process of *opening democracy*. This would include learning more about opportunities for alternative social constructions of human nature, including more understanding about the relationship of domination to antisocial behavior.

Chomsky has expressed this more concisely in his comment that, in his view, anarchism "is an expression of the idea that the burden of proof is always on those who argue that authority and domination are necessary. They have to demonstrate, with powerful argument, that the conclusion is correct. If they cannot, then the information they defend should be considered illegitimate. How one should react to illegitimate authority depends on circumstances and conditions: there are no formulas" (Lane, 1996).

In the Tradition

Talk of the process of a citizen turn and citizen-ing would be in a long tradition of political thinking throughout American and other histories. There have been various manifestations and interconnections. A citizen turn is similar to many visions not only in anarchist but also, for example, in ecological, feminist, and discourse thinking. It also connects with those who want to move from an *artificial* to a *natural* aristocracy, like Thomas Jefferson quoted above. Examples of artificial hierarchy could include one that privileges the rich merely because they are rich, or one that hires the boss's incompetent friend just because he is the boss's good friend.

"Where is our republicanism to be found?" asked Jefferson. His answer was, "Not in the constitution certainly, but merely in the spirit of our people" (Jefferson, 1884, 1305–1306; Brudney, 1992). The concern was reflected in the debates between the Federalists and Antifederalists like Patrick Henry. These debates included disagreement over Montesquieu's claim that large republics corrupt democratic virtue, for example. The concern has not been limited to a focus on republican or civic virtue, however. An example is the important literature and interest in civil society.

Concern with citizen spirit and relations has been the subject of empirical and other study, often under overlapping headings such as civil society, volunteerism, trust, or citizen engagement (e.g., Pew Research Center, 1996). An example is Robert Putnam's essay "Bowling Alone" (Putnam, 2000). Putnam argued that the vibrancy of American civil society has declined over the past thirty years, and he measured this not only in such terms as voter turnout and voluntary organization membership but also in (a questionable set of measures in our changing times) fewer bowling leagues and more individual bowling.

Talk of a citizen turn would also be in the tradition of the many varieties of the civil society perspective often seen as originating in the Scottish Enlightenment, and Adam Ferguson, Francis Hutcheson, and Adam Smith wrote in this way. Walzer (1995) describes the scene. The change of direction here is toward a private ethic, a move from virtue toward individual sociability or benevolence. This is not to suggest that the earlier tradition is replaced; for instance, Hannah Arendt and Alasdair MacIntyre write in the civic virtue tradition. Georg Hegel and Antonio Gramsci are among others who have also contributed to theorizing about those organizations that lie between the domains of the familial and the state, and Tocqueville rejoiced in the vibrancy and profusion of civil association. Walzer also points out that some would argue that these two traditions of thought are irreconcilable, and they would describe the contemporary debate between the liberal and republican versions of citizenship as a reformulation of the opposing traditions (e.g., Seligman, 1995). On one account, liberal theory thinks of the morally autonomous individual, each responsible for her own idea of the good life, and of the working of universally valid principles of justice. The republican version thinks of the polis as a moral community concerned to pursue a common good, where (as in Aristotle) the community is logically prior to the individual. Some thinkers draw on both traditions, as in post-communist societies.

Celebrating the centrality of citizen discourse for democracy, Habermas points (by implication) to the practical importance of a citizen turn. Habermas's more recent *Between Facts and Norms* (1996) continues his thinking by rejecting what he calls "liberal" (grounded in Hobbes) and "civic republican" (rooted in Aristotle and Rousseau) democracies. He favors "deliberative democracy," with an emphasis on activities like mutual consultative discourse and shared meanings rather than on implementing summed preferences. Earlier in his *Theory of Communicative Action,* Habermas (1987) has explained "communicatively shared intersubjectivity." He has also analyzed social evolution in terms of the decoupling of system and lifeworld. Habermas's view of the priority of communicative action includes the idea that such action not merely "should" be primary. Rather, it is that communicative action in fact "has" priority; the action is inevitably emancipatory and re-generative.

The regulative ideal of a citizen turn is an optimistic, and humanist, civic ideology. Our minds instantly (mis)jump to the phrase "we the people." Political governance becomes less a matter of relating-down, dealing-down, and governing-down. Governance in all its aspects is less and less explored and understood within a context of hierarchy—oligarchic, plutocratic, priestly, male-stream, disciplinary, and kingly. The citizen turn aims toward a killing, piece by piece, of the king.

References

Ackerman, Diane (1995). *A natural history of love.* New York: Vintage Books.
Adams, Irwin (1993). Heroines of peace: The nine Nobel women. www.nobel.se/peace/articles/heriones/index.html; July 1.
Adorno, Theodor (1981). *Prisms.* Cambridge, MA: MIT Press.
Agamben, Giorgio (1993). *Stanzas: Word and phantasm in western culture.* Minneapolis: University of Minnesota Press.
———— (1993a). *The coming community.* Minneapolis: University of Minnesota Press.
Albert, Michael (2003). *Parecon: Life after capitalism.* New York: Verso.
American Assembly (2001). *Racial equality: Public policies for the twenty-first century.* www.americanassembly.org.
American Psychiatric Association (2000). *Diagnostic and statistical manual of mental disorders.* 4th ed. Washington, DC: American Psychiatric Association.
Anscombe, Elizabeth (1958). Modern moral philosophy. *Philosophy* 33(4).
Apel, Karl O. (1981). Intention, conventions, and references to things. In Herman Parret & Jacques Bouveresse, *Meaning and understanding.* New York: de Gruyter.
Arestis, Philip & Malcolm Sawyer (2001). *A biographical dictionary of dissenting economists.* Williston, VT: Edward Elgar.
Arrow, Kenneth (1963). *Social choice and individual values.* 2nd ed. New York: Wiley.
Baechler, Jean (1975). *The origins of capitalism.* Oxford, UK: Blackwell.
Barry, Brian (1995). *Justice as impartiality.* Oxford: Clarendon Press.
Barthes, Roland (1978). *A lover's discourse: Fragments.* New York: Hill and Wang.
Barker, Ernest (1958). *The politics of Aristotle.* New York: Oxford University Press.
Bhabha, Homi (1994). *The location of culture.* London: Routledge.
Bloom, Harold (1998). *Shakespeare: The invention of the human.* New York: Riverhead Books.
———— (2000). *How to read and why.* New York: Scribner.
Blumer, Herbert (1969). *Symbolic interactionism: Perspective and method.* Englewood Cliffs, NJ: Prentice Hall.
Bonner, Neil (2004). www.michelangelo.com/buonarroti.html; March 17.
Box, Richard (2000). Pragmatic discourse and administrative legitimacy. *American Review of Public Administration* 32(1): 20–39.

—————— (2001). Private lives and anti-administration. *Administrative Theory & Praxis* 23(4): 541–558.

—————— (2003). Contradiction, utopia, and public administration. *Administrative Theory & Praxis* 25(2): 243–260.

Boyd, Richard & Philip Gasper (1993). *The philosophy of science.* Cambridge, MA: MIT Press.

Branagh, Kenneth (2004). www.branaghcompendium.com/conspiracy.html; April 4.

Brudney, Kent (1992). Machiavellian lessons in America: Republican findings, original principles, and political empowerment, 13–26. In Wilson Carey McWilliams & Michael T. Gibbons, *The Federalists, The Antifederalists, and the American Political Tradition.* New York: Greenwood Press.

Buchanan, Allen (1980). A critical introduction to Rawls' theory of justice. In H. Gene Blocker & Elizabeth Smith, *John Rawls' theory of social justice: An introduction.* Athens: Ohio University Press.

—————— (1991). Efficiency arguments for and against the market. In John Arthur & William Shaw, *Justice and economic distribution.* Englewood Cliffs, NJ: Prentice Hall.

Burke, Kenneth (1966). *Language as symbolic action.* Berkeley and Los Angeles: University of California Press.

—————— (1969). *A rhetoric of motives.* Berkeley and Los Angeles: University of California Press.

Burrell, Gibson (1997). *Pandemonium: Toward a retro-organization theory.* Thousand Oaks, CA: Sage.

Caldicott, Helen (2002). *The new nuclear danger: George W. Bush's military-industrial complex.* New York: New Press.

Campbell, Roy & Andrew Skinner (1976). *Adam Smith: An inquiry into the nature and the causes of the wealth of nations.* Oxford, UK: Clarendon Press.

Carniawska, Barbara (2000). *Writing management: Organization theory as a literary genre.* New York: Oxford University Press.

Carrette, Jeremy (2000). *Foucault and religion: Spiritual corporality and political spirituality.* London: Routledge.

Chalcraft, David (1994). Bringing the text back in: On ways of reading the iron cage metaphor in the two editions of The Protestant Ethic, 16–45. In Larry Ray & Michael Reed, *Organizing modernity: New Weberian perspectives on work, organizations, and society.* London: Routledge.

Champy, James (1995). *Reengineering management: The mandate for new leadership.* New York: HarperBusiness.

Chung, Sung (1997). Private correspondence, March 13, 1997.

Cixous, Hélène (1980). The laugh of the Medusa. In Elaine Marks & Isabelle De Coutivron, *New French feminisms: An anthology,* 245–264. Amherst: University of Massachusetts Press.

Clarke, Richard (2004). *Against all enemies: Inside America's war on terror.* New York: Free Press.

Coase, Ronald (1988). *The firm, the market, and the law.* Chicago: University of Chicago Press.

Cohen, Jean & Andrew Arato (1990). *Civil society.* Cambridge, MA: MIT Press.

Coleman, James (1974). *Power and structure of society.* New York: W.W. Norton.

Cooper, Richard (2003). *General casts war in religious terms.* www.commondreams.org/headlines03/10 16–01.htm; October 16.

Cornell, Drucilla, et al. (1992). *Deconstruction and the possibility of justice.* New York: Routledge.

Crosby, Michael (2003). A story about difference. *Clinical Society News,* 12(4). Richmond, VA: Virginia Society for Clinical Social Work.

Cunningham, Robert & Robert Schneider (2001). Anti-administration: Redeeming bureaucracy by witnessing and gifting. *Administrative Theory & Praxis* 23(4): 573–588.

Cupit, Geoffrey (1996). *Justice as fittingness.* Oxford: Clarendon Press.

Czarniawska, Barbara (1999). Writing management: Organization theory as a literary genre. New York: Oxford University Press.

———— (2004). Narratives in social science research. Thousand Oaks, CA: Sage.

Dandeker, Christopher (1990). *Surveillance, power and modernity: Bureaucracy and discipline from 1700 to the present day.* Cambridge, UK: Polity Press.

Dauenhauer, Bernard (1996). *Citizenship in a fragile world.* Lanham, MD: Rowman & Littlefield.

DeBuwitz, William (2004). www.ebeltz.net/resume/jir.html; April 1.

Deleuze, Gilles & Felix Guattari (1977). *Anti-Oedipus: Capitalism and schizophrenia.* New York: Viking Press.

———— (1987). *A thousand plateaus.* Minneapolis: University of Minnesota Press.

Denhardt, Kathryn (1991). *The ethics of public service: Resolving moral dilemmas in public organizations.* Westport, CT: Greenwood Press.

Derrida, Jacques (1979). *Spurs: Nietzsche's styles.* Chicago: University of Chicago Press.

———— (1998). Letter to a Japanese friend. In David Wood and Robert Bernasconi, *Derrida and difference.* Evanston, IL: Northwestern University Press.

Diesing, Paul (1991). *How does social science work? Reflections on practice.* Pittsburgh: University of Pittsburgh Press.

Donaldson, Stephen (1993). www.vix.com/pub/men/abuse/usa-prison.html; November 11.

Dunn, John (1984). The concept of 'trust' in the politics of John Locke, 279–301. In Richard Rorty, Jerome Schneewind & Quentin Skinner, *Philosophy in history.* New York: Cambridge University Press.

Edelman, Murray (1971). *Politics as symbolic action.* New York: Academic Press.

Eibl-Eibesfeldt, Irenaus (1982). *Love and hate.* New York: Holt, Rinehart and Winston.

Eribon, Didier (1991). *Michel Foucault.* Cambridge, MA: Harvard University Press.

Evans, Dylan (1996). *An introductory dictionary of Lacanian psychoanalysis.* New York: Routledge.

Farmer, David John (1984). *Crime control: The use and misuse of police resources.* New York: Plenum Press.

———— (1990). *Being in time: The nature of time in light of McTaggart's paradox.* Lanham, MD: University Press of America.

———— (1995). *The language of public administration: Bureaucracy, modernity, and postmodernity.* Tuscaloosa: University of Alabama Press.

————— (1998). Public administration discourse as play, 37–56. In David John Farmer, *The art of anti-administration*. Burke, VA: Chatelaine Press.

————— (2000). Public administration discourse: A matter of style? *Administration and Society* 31(3): 299–320.

————— (2001). Mapping anti-administration: Introduction to the symposium. *Administrative Theory & Praxis* 23(4): 475–492.

————— (2001a). Somatic writing: Attending to our bodies. *Administrative Theory & Praxis* 23(2): 187–204.

————— (2001b). Medusa: Hélène Cixous and the writing of laughter. *Administrative Theory & Praxis* 23(4): 559–572.

————— (2001c). Introduction, 87–90, 125–129. In David John Farmer, Camilla Stivers, Ralph Hummel, Cheryl King, & Sandra Kensen, Constructing civil space. *Administration and Society* 34(1): 87–129.

————— (2002). Discourses of anti-administration, 271–288. In Jong S. Jun, *Rethinking administrative theory: The challenge of the new century*. Westport, CT: Praeger.

————— (2002a). The devil's rope. *Administrative Theory & Praxis* 24(4): 781–786.

————— (2002b). Administrative love and un-engineering. *Administrative Theory & Praxis* 24(2): 369–380.

————— (2003). In the pink. *Administrative Theory & Praxis* 25(3): 419–426.

————— (2003a). The allure of rhetoric and the truancy of poetry. *Administrative Theory & Praxis* 25(1): 9–13.

————— (2003b). Power of refusal. *Administrative Theory & Praxis* 25(2 June): 173–183.

Farmer, David John & Patricia Patterson (2003). The reflective practitioner and the uses of rhetoric. *Public Administration Review* 63(1): 65–71.

Farmer, David John & Rosemary Lee Farmer (1997). Leopards in the temple: Bureaucracy and the limits of the in-between. *Administration and Society* 29(5 November): 507–528.

Farmer, Rosemary Lee (1999). Clinical HBSE concentration: A transactional model. *Journal of Social Work Education* 3(2): 289–299. Spring–Summer.

Farmer, Rosemary Lee (1997). Scenes from the unconscious. *Public Voices* 3(1 July): 67–81.

Feldman, Ruth, Arthur Eidelman, Lea Sirota, & Aron Weller (2002). Comparison of skin-to-skin (kangaroo) and traditional care: Parenting outcomes and preterm infant development. *Pediatrics* 110(1) July: 16–26.

Fincham, Robin (2000). Management as magic: Reengineering and the search for business salvation, 174–191. In D. Knights and H. Wilmott, *The Reengineering Revolution*. London: Sage.

Fogarty, Daniel (1959). *Roots for a new rhetoric*. New York: Teachers College of Columbia University.

Fogel, Robert (2000). *The fourth great awakening and the future of egalitarianism*. Chicago: University of Chicago Press.

Foucault, Michel (1966). *The order of things: An archaeology of the human sciences*. New York: Random House.

————— (1972). The archaeology of knowledge. New York: Pantheon.

————— (1977). Preface. In Gilles Deleuze and Felix Guattari, *Anti-Oedipus: Capitalism and schizophrenia*. New York: Viking Press.

—————— (1977a). *Discipline and punish: The birth of the prison.* New York: Pantheon.

—————— (1980). *Power/Knowledge: Selected interviews and other writings, 1972–1977.* Brighton, UK: Harvester Press.

Fraser, Nancy, et al. (1991). The uses and abuses of French discourse theories for feminist politics. In Philip Wexler, *Critical theory now.* London: Falmer Press.

Freud, S. (1961). *Civilization and its discontents.* New York: W.W. Norton.

—————— (1961a). *Beyond the pleasure principle.* New York: W.W. Norton.

—————— (1975). *The future of an illusion.* New York: W.W. Norton.

Gadamer, Hans Georg (1975). *Truth and method.* New York: Seabury.

—————— (1984). The Hermeneutics of suspicion, 54–65. In Gary Shapiro and Alan Sica, *Hermeneutics.* Amherst: University of Massachusetts Press.

—————— (1989). Text and interpretation, 21–51. In Diane Michelfelder and Richard Palmer, *Dialogue and deconstruction.* Albany, NY: SUNY Press.

Galston, William (1991). Liberal purposes: Goods, virtues, and diversity in the liberal state. New York: Cambridge University Press.

Gibran, Kahlil (1995). *Sand and foam: A book of aphorisms.* New York: A.A. Knopf.

Gilligan, Carol (1982). *In a different voice: Psychological theory and women's development.* Cambridge, MA: Harvard University Press.

Goodman, Nelson (1978). *Ways of worldmaking.* Indianapolis: Hackett.

Gould, James (1963). The not-so-golden rule. *Southern Journal of Philosophy* 1 (Fall): 10–14.

Graham, Angus (1992). *Unreason within reason: Essays on the outskirts of rationality.* LaSalle, IL: Open Court.

Greenhouse, Steven (2004). Workers assail night lock-ins by Wal-Mart, 1 & 24. *New York Times,* January 18.

—————— (2004a). Altering of worker time cards spurs growing number of suits, 1 & 16. *New York Times,* April 4.

Gulick, Luther & Lyndall Urwick (1937). *Papers on the science of administration.* New York: Institute of Public Administration.

Habermas, Jürgen (1971). *Knowledge and human interests.* Shapiro, trans. Boston: Beacon Press.

—————— (1983). Modernity: An incomplete project. In Hal Foster, *The Anti-Aesthetic: Essays on postmodern culture.* Port Townsend, WA: Bay Press.

—————— (1987). *Theory of communicative action.* Boston, MA: Beacon Press.

—————— (1996). *Between facts and norms: Contributions to a discourse theory of law and democracy.* Cambridge, MA: MIT Press.

Hadot, Pierre (1995). *Philosophy as a way of life: Spiritual exercise from Socrates to Foucault.* Oxford, UK: Blackwell.

Hall, Calvin & Gardner Lindzey (1957). *Theories of personality.* New York: John Wiley & Sons.

Hare, Richard (1989). *Essays in ethical theory.* New York: Oxford University Press.

Harter, Pascale (2004). www.news.bbc.co.uk/2/hi/Africa/3429903.htm; January 26.

Heidegger. Martin (1969/1972). *On time and being.* New York: Harper & Row.

—————— (1971). *On the way to language.* New York: Harper & Row.

Henwood, Doug (2003). *After the new economy.* New York: New Press.

Hermans, Hubert & Harry Kempen (1993). *The dialogical self: Meaning as movement.* New York: Academic Press.

Hobbes, Thomas (1991). *Leviathan.* New York: Cambridge University Press.

hooks, bell (2002). *Communion: The female search for love.* New York: HarperCollins.

Howe, Louis (2003). Ontology and refusal in subaltern ethics. *Administrative Theory & Praxis* 25(2): 277–298.

Hutchinson, Janet (2001). Multigendering PA: Anti-administration, anti-blues. *Administrative Theory & Praxis* 23(4): 589–604.

Ignatieff, Michael (1984). *The needs of strangers.* New York: Henry Holt.

Jacobs, Debra (2001). Alterity and the environment: Making the case for anti-administration. *Administrative Theory & Praxis* 23(4): 605–620.

Jefferson, Thomas (1884). *Writings.* New York: Library of America.

Joyce, J. (1997). *Ulysses.* London: Macmillan.

Kaminski, June & Wendy Hall (1996). The effect of soothing music on neonatal behavior states in the hospital newborn nursery. *Neonatal Network* 15(1 February): 45–54.

Kant, Immanuel (1950). *Foundations of the metaphysics of morals.* Chicago, IL: University of Chicago Press.

——— (1957). What is enlightenment? In Lewis White, *On history.* Indianapolis: Bobbs-Merrill.

——— (1997). *Critique of practical reason.* New York: Cambridge University Press.

Kaplan, Harold, Benjamin Sadock & Jack Grebb (2003). *Synopsis of psychiatry: Behavioral sciences clinical psychiatry.* Baltimore, MD: Williams & Wilkins.

Kelly, Marjorie (2001). *The divine right of capital: Dethroning the corporate aristocracy.* San Francisco, CA: Berrett-Koehler Publishers.

Kennickell, Arthur. (2003). A rolling tide: Changes in the distribution of wealth in the U.S., 1989–2001; www.federalreserve.gov/pubs/oss/oss2/scfindex.html. Retrieved August 2004.

Kensen, Sandra (2000). The dialogue as basis for democratic governance. *Administrative Theory & Praxis* 22(1): 117–131.

King, Cheryl & Sandra Kensen (2002). Associational public space: Politics, administration, and storytelling, 108–113. In David John Farmer et al., Constructing civil space: A dialogue, *Administration and Society* 34(1): 87–129.

Korton, David (2001). *When corporations rule the world.* West Hartford, CT: Kumarian Press.

Krugman, Paul (2002). For richer: How the permissive capitalism of the boom destroyed American equality, 62–142. *New York Times Magazine*, October 20.

Kundera, Milan (1996). *The book of laughter and forgetting.* New York: HarperCollins.

Kymlicka, Will (1990). *Contemporary political philosophy: An introduction.* Oxford: Clarendon Press.

Lacan, Jacques (1977). *Ecrits.* New York: W.W. Norton.

Lacey, Robert & Danny Danziger (2000). *The year 1000: What life was like at the turn of the first millennium.* London: Abacus.

Laing, R.D. (1970). *Knots.* London: Tavistock Publications.

Landesman, Peter (2004). The girls next door, 32–75. *New York Times Magazine,* January 25.

Lane, Tom (1996). Noam Chomsky on anarchism. www.zmag.org/chomsky/interviews/9612/anarchism.html; December 23.

Laporte, Dominique (1993). *History of shit.* Cambridge, MA: MIT Press.

Lau, D.C. (1979). *Confucius: The analects.* New York: Penguin Books.

Legge, James (1960). *The Chinese classics, I: Confucian analects, the great learning, the doctrine of the mean.* Hong Kong: Hong Kong University Press.

LePoidevan, Robin (1991). Review of 'Being in Time.' *Mind* (July).

Levy, C.J. (2002). Mentally ill and locked away in nursing homes in New York. *New York Times,* October 6, p. 1, col. 1–3.

———. (2002a). For mentally ill, death and misery. *New York Times,* April 28, p. 1, col. 4–6.

Lewis, Bernard (2002). *What went wrong? Western impact and Middle Eastern response.* New York: Oxford University Press.

Lewis, Carol (1991). *The ethics challenge in public service: A problem-solving guide.* San Francisco, CA: Jossey-Bass.

Locke, John (1988). *The second treatise of government.* New York: Cambridge University Press.

Loh, Michael (1997). *Re-engineering at work.* Aldershot, UK: Gower.

Lyotard, Jean-Francois (1984). Rewriting modernity. *SubStance* 54: 8–9.

——— (1991). *The inhuman: Reflections on time.* Stanford, CA: Stanford University Press.

Mandeville, Bernard (1714/1970). *Fable of the bees.* London: Penguin.

Marcuse, Herbert (1955). *Eros and civilization.* Boston: Beacon Press.

——— (1991). *One-dimensional man: Studies in the ideology of advanced industrial society.* Boston, MA: Beacon Press.

Margalit, Avishai (1996). *The decent society.* Cambridge, MA: Harvard University Press.

Martin, Hans-Peter & Harald Schumann (1998). *The global trap: Globalization and the assault on democracy and prosperity.* New York: Zed Books.

Mates, Benson (1996). *The skeptic way: Sextus Empiricus's outlines of pyrrhonism.* New York: Oxford University Press.

McClosky, Deidre (1998). *The rhetoric of economics.* 2nd ed. Madison: University of Wisconsin Press.

——— (2001). The genealogy of postmodernism: An economist's guide, 102–128. In Stephen Cullenberg, Jack Amariglio & David Ruccio, *Postmodernism, economics, and knowledge.* New York: Routledge.

McSwite, O.C. (1997). Postmodernism and public administration's identity crisis. *Public Administration Review* 55(12) (March): 174–181.

——— (1997a). *Legitimacy in public administration: A discourse analysis.* Thousand Oaks, CA: Sage Publications.

——— (1998). Stories from the 'real world'; Administering anti-administratively. In David John Farmer, *Papers on the art of anti-administration.* Burke, VA: Chatelaine Press.

——— (2000). On the discourse movement: A self interview. *Administrative Theory & Praxis* 22(1): 45–48.

————— (2001). The psychoanalytic rationale for anti-administration. *Administrative Theory & Praxis* 23(4) (December): 493–506.

————— (2003). Now more than ever—refusal as redemption. *Administrative Theory & Praxis* 25(2): 183–404.

Merleau-Ponty, Maurice (1962). *Phenomenology of perception.* London: Routledge and Kegan Paul.

Mill, John Stuart (1961). On liberty. In Marshall Cohen, *The philosophy of John Stuart Mill.* New York: Modern Library.

Misztal, Barbara (1988). *Trust in modern societies.* Cambridge, UK: Polity Press.

Monk, Ray (1996). *Bertrand Russell: The spirit of solitude.* New York: Free Press.

Moravec, Hans (1998). *Robot: Mere machines in transcendent mind.* New York: Oxford University Press.

More, Thomas (1949). *Utopia.* Northbrook, IL: AHM Publishing.

Morris, D. & J. Brandon (1993). *Reengineering your business.* New York: McGraw-Hill.

Mueller, Dennis (2003). *Public choice III.* New York: Cambridge University Press.

Nagel, Ernest & James Newman (1958). *Godel's proof.* New York: New York University Press.

Nemeth, Elisabeth & Friedrich Stadler (2002). *Encyclopedia and utopia: The life and work of Otto Neurath (1882–1945).* New York: Kluwer Academic Publishers.

Newman, John Henry (1979). *An essay in aid of a grammar of assent.* Notre Dame, IN: University of Notre Dame Press.

Nietzsche, Friedrich (1968). *Twilight of the idols.* Baltimore, MD: Penguin Books.

————— (1989). *Beyond good and evil: A prelude to a philosophy of the future.* New York: Vintage Books.

9/11 Commission (2004). *Final report of the national commission on terrorist attacks upon the United States.* New York: W.W. Norton.

Niskanen, William (1971). *Bureaucracy and representative government.* Chicago: Aldine-Atherton.

Novalis (2000). When geometric diagrams. Trans. R. Bly. In The poet's tree: A celebration of poetry. p. 1. Retrieved February 16, 2003, from www.geocities.com/Paris/Pavillion/1467/files/westNovalis.html.

Nozick, Robert (1974). Anarchy, state, and utopia, 61–102. In John Arthur and William Shaw, *Justice and economic distribution.* Englewood Cliffs, NJ: Prentice Hall.

Nussbaum, Martha (1990). *Love's knowledge: Essays on philosophy and literature.* New York: Oxford University Press.

Oakeshott, Michael (1991). The voice of poetry in the conversation of mankind, 488–541. In *Rationalism in politics and other essays.* Indianapolis, IN: Liberty Fund.

Offe, Claus, et al. (1991). Democratic institutions and moral resources, 143–171. In David Held, *Political theory today.* Cambridge, UK: Polity Press.

Oldstone-Moore, Jennifer (2002). *Confucianism: Origins, beliefs, practices, holy texts, sacred places.* New York: Oxford University Press.

Pagels, Elaine (1981). *The gnostic gospels.* New York: Vintage Books.

Palast, Greg (2003). *The best democracy money can buy: An investigative reporter exposes the truth about globalization, corporate cons, and high-finance fraudsters.* New York: Plume.

Patterson, Patricia (2000). Nonvirtue is not apathy: Warrants for discourse and citizen dissent. *American Review of Public Administration* 30(3): 225–251.

——— (2000a). The talking cure and the silent treatment: Some limits of 'discourse' as speech. *Administrative Theory & Praxis* 22(4): 663–695.

——— (2001). Imagining anti-administration's anti-hero (antagonist? protagonist? agonist?). *Administrative Theory & Praxis* 43(4): 529–540.

——— (2003). Interpretation, contradiction and refusal: The best lack all conviction? *Administrative Theory & Praxis* 25(2): 233–242.

Pew Research Center (1996). *Trust and citizen engagement in metropolitan Philadelphia*. Washington, DC: Pew Research Center for the People and the Press.

Putnam, Robert (2000). *Bowling alone: The collapse and revival of American community*. New York: Simon & Schuster.

Rauschning, Hermann (1941). *The redemption of democracy: The coming Atlantic empire*. New York: Literary Guild of America.

Rawls, John (1971). *A theory of justice*. Cambridge, MA: Harvard University Press.

——— (1993). *Political liberalism*. New York: Columbia University Press.

Rein, M. (1976). *Social science and public policy*. New York: Penguin.

Reiner, Hans (1983). *Duty and inclination: The fundamentals of morality discussed and refined with special regard to Kant and Schiller*. Boston, MA: Martinus Nijhoff Publishers.

Richards, Ivor (1936/1965). *The philosophy of rhetoric*. New York: Oxford University Press.

Ricoeur, Paul (1990). The golden rule: Exegetical and theological perplexities. *New Testament Studies* 36: 392–397.

Rothschild, E. (2001). *Economic sentiments: Adam Smith, condorcet, and the enlightenment*. Cambridge, MA: Harvard University Press.

Russell, Bertrand (1959). *The problems of philosophy*. Oxford: Oxford University Press.

Said, Edward (1978). *Orientalism*. New York: Pantheon Books.

Samuelson, Paul & William Nordhaus (1989). *Economics*. 13th ed. New York: McGraw-Hill.

Scott, James (1990). *Domination and the arts of resistance: Hidden transcripts*. New Haven, CT: Yale University Press.

Seligman, Adam (1992) *The idea of civil society*. New York: Free Press.

——— (1995). Animadversion upon civil society and civic virtue in the last decade of the twentieth century, 200–223. In John Hall, *Civil society: Theory, history, comparison*. Cambridge, UK: Polity Press.

Shapiro, Michael (1993). *Reading 'Adam Smith': Desire, history and value*. Newbury Park, CA: Sage Publications.

Short, Jennifer (2004). Can a trial lawyer expose Saudi complicity in terrorism? *New York Times Magazine,* March 14, p. 39.

Simon, Herbert (1945/1976). *Administrative behavior: A study of decision-making processes in administrative organization*. 3rd ed. New York: Free Press.

——— (1991). *Models of my life*. Cambridge, MA: MIT Press.

Singer, Marcus (1967). Golden rule, 365–367. *The encyclopedia of philosophy*. New York: Macmillan.

Singer, Peter (1981). *The expanding circle: Ethics and sociobiology*. New York: Farrar, Straus & Giroux.

Smart, John (1991). Distributive justice and utilitarianism, 106–117. In John Arthur and William Shaw, *Justice and economic distribution*. Englewood Cliffs, NJ: Prentice Hall.

Smart, John & Bernard Williams (1973). *Utilitarianism for and against*. Cambridge: Cambridge University Press.

Solomon, Robert & Mark Murphy (1990). *What is justice? Classic and contemporary readings*. New York: Oxford University Press.

Sorensen, Roy (1992). *Thought experiments*. New York: Oxford University Press.

Spicer, Michael (2001). Value pluralism and its implications for American public administration. *Administrative Theory & Praxis* 23(4): 507–528.

Springer, John (2004). *Before and after treatment, stoning mother displayed contrasting emotions*. www.courttv.com/trials/Laney/040104_ctv.html; May 2.

Stemple, Lara (2002). www.spr.org/en/pressreleases/pr_02_081402.html; December 24.

Stiglitz, Joseph (2002). *Globalization and its discontents*. New York: W.W. Norton.

——— (2003). *The roaring nineties: A new history of the world's most prosperous decade*. New York: W.W. Norton.

Stone, Deborah (2001). *Policy paradox: The art of political decision making*. New York: HarperCollins.

Taylor, Charles (1985). Interpretation and the sciences of man. In *Philosophical Papers*, vol. 2, *Philosophy and the Human Sciences*. Cambridge: Cambridge University Press.

Tocqueville, Alexis de (1999). *Democracy in America*. New York: Westvaco.

Torres, Carol, Diane Halditch-Davis, Ann O'Hale & Jennifer D'Auria (1997). Effect of standard rest periods on apnea and weight gain in preterm infants. *Neonatal Network* 16(8): 35–43.

Town, Sarah (2004). www.inmotionmagazine.com/mariel.htm; March 15.

Twigg, Judith (2003). Personal communication. March 1.

Walzer, Michael (1983). *Spheres of justice*. New York: Basic Books.

——— (1995). The concept of civil society, 7–34. In Michael Walzer, *Toward a global civil society*. Oxford: Berghahn Books.

Warnke, Georgia (1993). *Justice and interpretation*. Cambridge, MA: MIT Press.

Weber, Max (1958). *The protestant ethic and the spirit of capitalism*. New York: Scribner's.

White, Jay (2000). Taking language seriously: The narrative foundation of public administration research. Washington, DC: Georgetown University Press.

Wisdom, John (1987). *Challengeability in modern science*. Aldershot, UK: Avebury.

Wittgenstein, Ludwig (1961). *Tractatus logico-philosophicus*. New York: Routledge.

Yanow, Dvora (2002). *Constructing race and ethnicity in America: Category-making in public policy and administration*. Armonk, New York: M.E. Sharpe.

Zanetti, Lisa (2003). Holding contradictions: Marcuse and the idea of refusal. *Administrative Theory & Praxis* 25(2): 261–276.

Index

A

Ackerman, Diane, 180
Administrative Behavior: A Study of Decision-Making Processes in Administrative Organizations (Simon), 13
administrative ethics, 79–80
administrative play. *See* thinking as play
Administrative Theory & Praxis (journal), 49
Adorno, Theodor, 69, 174
Against All Enemies: Inside America's War on Terror (Clarke), 23
Agamben, Giorgio, 17, 32, 40–41
agnosticism, 70
Albert, Michael, 165
Allegory of Good Government (Lorenzetti), 137
altruism, 117, 119
American Assembly, 25
American Public Administration, 55
Americans United for the Separation of Church and State, 91
Analects of Confucius, 122

anarchism, 163
anti-administration model, 28–31
  feminist perspective of, 30
Antisthenes, 48
Apel, Karl, 90
aporia, 1, 69, 76–77, 114
  definition of, 62
Aquinas, Thomas, 46
Arendt, Hannah, 193
arguments of others, 111–13
aristocracy, 192
aristocratic power, 162
Aristotle, 8, 40, 62, 76, 95, 117–18, 194
Arnold, Matthew, 36
Arrow, Kenneth, 188–89
ataraxia (peace of mind), 70
audit systems, 139
Augustine, 69, 104, 155
authentic hesitation, 103–7, 138–39
  antecedents of, 108
  in governance, 105
  justice-seeking and, 106
  moral principle motivation, 105

B

Barthes, Roland, 179
Between Facts and Norms (Habermas), 194

About the Author

David John Farmer is professor of government and public affairs, Virginia Commonwealth University. He received his bachelor of science degree from the London School of Economics and Political Science, University of London; a master's degree from the University of Toronto and a master's from the University of Virginia; a Ph.D. in economics from the University of London, and a Ph.D. in philosophy from the University of Virginia. He was employed by the city of New York and by the U.S. Department of Justice. His is author of *Crime Control: The Use and Misuse of Police Resources* (1984), *Being in Time: The Nature of Time in Light of McTaggart's Paradox* (1990), *The Language of Public Administration: Bureaucracy, Modernity, and Postmodernity* (1995), and he is the editor of *The Art of Anti-Administration* (1998).